Classroom Management

A Resource Manual for Frontline Teachers

Ray Petty

The Scarecrow Press, Inc.
Scarecrow Education
Lanham, Maryland, and London
2001

SCARECROW PRESS, INC.
A Scarecrow Education Book

Published in the United States of America
by Scarecrow Press, Inc.
4720 Boston Way
Lanham, Maryland 20706
www.scarecrowpress.com

4 Pleydell Gardens, Folkestone
Kent CT20 2DN, England

British Library Cataloguing-in-Publication Information Available

Library of Congress Cataloging-in-Publication Data

Petty, Ray, 1944–
    Classroom management : a resource manual for frontline teachers /
    Ray Petty.   p. cm. — (A Scarecrow education book)
    ISBN 0-8108-4078-2 (pbk. : alk. paper)
    1. Classroom management—Handbooks, manuals, etc. I. Title. II. Series.
    LB3013 .P45 2001
    371.102'4—dc21   2001031078

∞™ The paper used in this publication meets the minimum requirements
of American National Standard for Information Sciences—Permanence of
Paper for Printed Library Materials, ANSI/NISO Z39.48-1992.
Manufactured in the United States of America.

Illustrations by Robert Gallagher

This book is also available in Spanish: Puede adquirirse en español de
Publicaciones Puertorriqueñas, San Juan, Puerto Rico, ISBN 1-881713-73-3

Contents

Acknowledgments

I would like to express my appreciation to Mary T. Finn, Teresa Carew, Elizabeth Michaelis, Edna Negrón, Ann Price, and Edward Weinswig, and members of my school staff who provided important input and collegial encouragement. And special thanks to the kids—they taught me most of what I know.

Introduction

While the skills of discipline and classroom management are the foundations of good teaching, many still cling to the archaic belief that teachers are born with them. It is only recently that we have come to realize that they are not. Just as mothers and fathers are not necessarily born with good parenting skills, teachers do not enter their first year of teaching with innate skills in classroom management and discipline. Of even more concern, many teacher-training institutions, if they address it at all, pay brief attention to the development of these skills. They spend three semester hours on the "History of Education" and not three minutes on an organized presentation on classroom management. Consequently, many of our teacher preparation institutions turn out exquisite mathematicians who can't peel students off the wall and gifted grammarians who go home at night pulling spitballs from their hair.

In 1968 I entered the classroom, as teacher, for the first time. Putting it politely, my first year was a disaster! I was on a continual guilt trip. I tried to perpetuate the American system by creating a democracy within my classroom, constantly closing the doors to keep the chaos within. I felt terrible about much of what was going on. I have now had sufficient educational experience to understand that I had a typical "first year." In fact, there are very few beginning teachers who are really good. Most find their first year a time to reassess and reevaluate many basic tenets. Much of our idealism about teaching and the styles developed from that idealism are quickly tempered by the realities of life as taught to us by our students. We learn how it feels to be manipulated, how exquisite lesson plans can fall apart with a sneeze, and how the classroom role of "benevolent dictator" is essential to the continuation of an educated democracy.

In 1978 I was given the opportunity to start a special school within the Hartford (Connecticut) public school system for students with significant violent and acting-out behavior. Starting with one teacher, an aide, and the five most violent students from a population of 26,000, we began to develop an educational approach for students who tried the abilities of our colleagues in their mainstream schools. Since, at the time, there was very little specific research available to assist with this type of population, much of what we developed came from basic "parental common sense." Because the behaviors were so extreme and overt, it was easy to recognize them and develop appropriate intervention strategies. This book is based upon those experiences and is the result of a team approach within that school. Teachers, aides, and administration worked closely together in the development of these philosophies and strategies. While these important principles, concepts, and techniques were developed using this extreme population, they are appropriate with any student and can effectively be applied to every classroom.

While we constantly discuss education in terms of reading and mathematics growth, we lose sight of the fact that the primary function of public school education is to prepare students to be productive members of our society. The most important area in this preparation is the development of social skills and an appreciation for the rules by which a democracy is governed and managed. Yet we spend thousands of hours in the development of reading and mathematics curricula and little—if any—in the development of a social skills or discipline curricula. This book is a beginning step in that process.

It is not written to give specific answers to problems within a particular classroom. Educators learned a long time ago that one cannot transplant specific educational solutions from one classroom to another, let alone from one school to another. There are too many variables. Since the individual details of each classroom situation differ, there is no correct master plan. This book gives some philosophical and behavioral parameters within which to operate. It raises questions that need to be answered and demonstrates possible solutions based on their answers. It allows a teacher to apply much of what is already known from a different perspective.

If this book can help educators evaluate their classroom management and discipline skills and give them some new techniques to consider in these areas, it has accomplished its purpose. It is a commonsense resource manual for teachers on the front line of today's education.

CHAPTER 1

Basic Principles

There are basic principles that underpin appropriate classroom management and discipline. If these principles are understood and applied, any response in a specific situation will be appropriate when it fits within the principles' basic parameters. They are presented without regard to priority, as they exist simultaneously and in a symbiotic relationship.

US VS. THEM

There are only two groups within the school—adults and students. It is important that everyone understands this simple distinction. Every student is responsible to every adult. "You're not my teacher" is an inappropriate response. Every adult is responsible for every student. "He's not in my class" is equally inappropriate. Within the school environment, students must learn to respond appropriately to every adult, regardless of that adult's position. Likewise, each adult is responsible for each student, regardless of classroom assignment. In such a way, students learn that the adults in the school work together as a team, and efforts to play one adult against another are minimized.

To maintain this unity, staff members must work together to ensure that one role does not undercut another. They must see themselves as supportive members of a team and realize that team cooperation is essential to their task. When the principal intercedes in a situation and takes over for the teacher, the teacher can be rendered impotent. The same is true when the teacher intercedes with an aide. We must be careful to ensure that students understand that they are responsible to every adult in the school, regardless of that adult's status. Respecting the cafeteria aide is equally as important as respecting the superintendent of schools, and their word should carry equal weight with the student.

CREATE YOUR CAMELOT

You are royalty in your area of influence. If you are a teacher, it is your classroom. If you are a gym aide, it is the gym. If you are the principal, it encompasses the entire school community. As "king" or "queen," you are the ultimate authority within your area of influence. Your word is final, and the students must understand that. Further, as "monarch" you may make decisions with no need for justification. Although in reality each of us has superiors to whom we must respond, the students need never see that. In our relations with our students, we are the boss!

This authority relationship does not imply a strict, uncaring dictatorship. Classroom control and management is best accomplished within

a caring and warm ambience. Limits can be set with a smile. Consequences, both positive and negative, can come from a loving adult.

As "monarch" in our classroom, our actions and behavior become the role model, our lessons impart knowledge, and our word is law. Students look to us as an adult role model and as a fount of knowledge and understanding. In discipline, they must see us as the arresting officer, as the prosecutor, and as the circuit, appellate, and supreme court judge. The only time we need use democracy is when it is part of a carefully structured lesson. When the response to "Sit down" is "Why do I have to sit down? Johnny isn't sitting down," our appropriate response is a firm and direct "Sit down!" We owe no explanation to anyone in our kingdom. By responding with reasons we are probably playing into a manipulation by which the student has momentarily taken control of our class.

This does not mean that our classroom must resemble the cold confines of a prison ward. As second parents, educators can demonstrate a warm and caring environment. "Sit down!" can be said using a warm voice and a smile; limits can be set in a positive way. But it is our responsibility to set those limits. While the children may initially object and push to expand them, they actually appreciate limits as they provide for a secure environment—something that children seek.

To support this relationship, it is important that superiors who enter our classroom do not inadvertently topple us from our thrones. When an administrator enters a teacher's class during a problem situation, he or she must always be careful to allow the teacher to continue to direct the situation. The administrator does not take over, but provides assistance and support at the direction of the teacher. In this way, the teacher does not lose authority. In fact, the opposite is true. The students see the teacher directing the principal and react, "Did you see that? Miss Jones was telling the principal what to do!" Even if it is not said, it is felt, and this feeling enhances the teacher's authority within the classroom as in the following example.

Scenario: Jasmine has exhibited a particular inappropriate behavior several times. The teacher has dealt with it each time with increasingly severe consequences, but it continues. He now feels that he needs the principal's support to reinforce his authority with Jasmine and show her the seriousness of the problem. He meets in advance with the principal, explains the situation, and plans a strategy with him. The next time Jasmine exhibits the behavior, the teacher calls the office and the principal responds. They step out into the hall with Jasmine, and the following dialogue ensues.

Teacher: I have spoken with Jasmine about her continuing to call Mary names. I have reprimanded her several times, but she continues. I think that I am going to have to call her mother to advise her of the situation if it happens again.

Principal: That is serious. I agree with you that behavior like this must stop. Please let me know if it happens again, and I will cover your class while you make the call. You can use the phone in my office.

At this point Jasmine and the teacher return to class, and the principal goes back to the office. The teacher has maintained control and authority in the situation. The principal has added authority to that of the teacher. And Jasmine sees the authority of both teacher and principal joined together in response to the seriousness of her inappropriate behavior.

Let's look at the same scenario with an incorrect approach.

Teacher: I have spoken with Jasmine about her continuing to call Mary names. I have punished her several times, but she continues. I think that I am going to have to call her mother, to advise her of the situation, if it happens again.

Principal: Jasmine, is that true?

Jasmine: No! Mary called me a . . . blah . . . blah . . . blah.

Principal: Well Jasmine, I understand that but the teacher isn't going to lie to me. If this happens again, I will have to . . .

See the difference? By taking over in the situation, the principal has taken power from the teacher and placed him- or herself in the role of final authority. "If this happens again, I will have to . . . ." Unfortunate error for the teacher. The teacher has delegated final authority for a student within his or her classroom to a third party. Worse yet, the authority was taken from the teacher.

SETTING APPROPRIATE EXPECTATIONS

We understand the importance of setting high levels of academic expectation for our students. Studies have shown that, in reading for example, students will rise to the levels that we set. Conversely, when we set low levels of expectation, students make minimal progress. What we fail to realize is that the same is true for behaviors. Student behavior will rise to our level of expectation. And low expectations will result in lowered behavioral performance.

In addition to setting high behavioral expectations, it is very important that the teacher internalize those expectations. It is very easy to voice an expectation, while deep in our hearts we doubt it. Ultimately that doubt shows through our nonverbal communications, leaving the student with a lower level of expectation.

An interesting complexity to expectations is that we are a significant other for the student. We are important to him or her. Consequently, if we set a low behavioral expectation, the student will respond with that behavior so as not to let us down. Let me illustrate.

Mary has had serious behavioral problems for a long period of time. When she "goes off," she picks up a book and hurls it across the room. The teacher has learned to recognize the escalation of behaviors leading up to the book toss and dread them as they progress. Today Mary has a problem and the teacher sees the behaviors progressing. The teacher says, "Now Mary, don't pick up the book." Without realizing it, the teacher has set an expectation for Mary's behavior. The teacher expects that she is going to pick up the book. Maybe this is the first time she was consciously trying to control herself and refrain from throwing it. But as a significant other, the teacher has set an expectation. So as not to let the teacher down and make him or her look foolish, Mary picks up the book and gives it a good toss. The teacher's actions initiated the behavior!

This is also true for students with a history of serious, violent behavior such as teacher assaults. Regardless of their history, we must expect appropriate behavior from them at all times. Successive approximation in which swearing at you is viewed as an improvement over hitting you may demonstrate behavioral improvement. But we would never say, "Good job, you swore rather than hit!" We must set an expectation for appropriate behavior from all students at all times. You will find that because you expect it, you will generally get it. Amazing, but true.

CHAPTER 2

Professional Thoughts

THE 8 TO 4 PROFESSIONAL: LOVE DURING WORKING HOURS

To be a good educator, you must have a sincere concern for your pupils. As each student's "second parent," this concern is like parental love. And that love, if it is real, goes beyond the workday. Although no one advocates that you move in with each student for a week, it is important that you back up your concern by being there when the student needs you. Sometimes that requires going beyond the traditional school day. If you tell José that you really care about him, make sure you have time to talk with him when he calls you at home at 7:30 on a Saturday evening with what he sees as a pressing personal problem.

Speaking of the phone call, please leave your number in the telephone directory. How many times do teachers say that they have an unlisted number because they are worried about being continually bothered? Teachers with listed telephones are lucky if they get one school-related call a month. If an occasional harassing call is received, it's very easy to hang up.

EGO: DOWNFALL OF THE PROFESSIONAL

As teachers, we are part of the human race, with all of the characteristics of that species. But, as educators, we are also professionals, and that professional role requires that we rise above a "normal" human response in many situations. One such area calling for a professional response is in the control of our ego. How many times have we let our emotions take over? You smile when a student compliments you on what you're wearing. You frown when another student blames you for her failure on the exam because the questions weren't fair.

Educators must maintain a professional demeanor even when faced with an emotional situation. Did you ever wonder how a surgeon could open a chest, crack the ribs, and cut open the heart during open-heart surgery? We perceive the normal reaction would be to pass-out before the end of step one. The surgeon continues because of conditioning and training that overcomes human emotions in the performance of his or her professional duties. The teacher is no different.

In one school, an employee tried to do bodily harm to a student who had made reference to the staff member's mother and her alleged sexual habits. The staff member was frothing at the mouth and had to be restrained from hurting the student. The student, meanwhile, was in his glory. He had superbly manipulated the staff member and was obviously in control. Other employees talked with the staff member and, after some time, brought him to the realization that the student was playing on his emotions. The student did not know the mother, the staff member knew his mother was faithful, and the whole episode, when studied, was an ego explosion.

While it is regrettable, there are times when students will assault school staff members. When a student seriously assaults us, our immediate reaction may be to respond in kind. It is imperative, however, that we allow our intellect to maintain control over our emotions as we continue to act in a professional manner. While it is hopefully not the norm, we must be prepared for such actions on an occasional basis. (That does not mean that they are condoned.) Students learn appropriate behaviors by trial and error, just as they learn math from their mistakes. As an educator, you must be prepared to deal in a professional manner with their behavioral errors, making them learning experiences for the student.

FRIEND TO STUDENTS—LEAVE ME OUT

In today's society, most students have a large number of friends, but less have good authority figures. Consequently, it is important that teachers maintain their authority relationship. An important part of that relationship is teaching the student to address the teacher properly.

A teacher who allows or invites his or her students to refer to him or her on a first-name basis is confusing the relationship. Just as the priest is Father, the minister is Reverend, and the physician is Doctor, the teacher is Mr., Mrs., Miss, or Ms. The title is a demonstration of respect.

At the same time, it is important that students see the teacher not as a "buddy," but as a significant authority figure. During their first year of teaching, many teachers are bothered when the students appear to dislike them. They are in a perpetual popularity contest. It takes some time before they realize that they can't be both an authority figure and a "buddy." One contradicts the other. The proof comes when you see students returning to visit many years after graduation, and almost without fail, they visit the teachers known for their strict and tough standards. Those are the teachers remembered with respect.

While on this subject, it is important that we mention the teacher as role model. It is imperative that we set ourselves as examples for our students. Even though a teacher may have a colorful vocabulary by nature, he or she must try extremely hard to maintain appropriate vocabulary in front of students. Since we expect that behavior from them, it would be hypocritical for us to do otherwise. How unfortunate it is when the health teacher finishes a lesson on smoking with one breath as he or she rushes to the teachers' room for a cigarette with the next. Our greatest teaching technique is by example, and we must use it wisely.

THAT'S NOT MY SPECIALTY

As in medicine, education seems to have entered the age of specialization. Just as I remember going to Dr. Chamberlain for every ailment, so too do I remember Mrs. Harris providing for my entire sixth-grade educational needs. Now, however, times have changed. I see an orthopedic surgeon for a bone problem, the allergist for my runny nose (after a consultation with the ear, nose, and throat specialist), and the gastroenterologist for my stomach pains. The same is true in education. I see the teacher for class, the hall monitor as I go to the next class, the truant officer when I miss a day, the social worker for my family concerns, the guidance counselor for scheduling, the art teacher for his or her special subject, and the vice principal when I deviate from the behavioral norm. This does not take into account the unofficial hierarchy — the executive secretary in the main office when I need to skirt the system and the custodian when I need some special supplies.

Fortunately, we are beginning to see the reemergence of the General Practitioner in medicine. Hopefully, the return of the General Educator cannot be far behind. In our system of dividing responsibilities, we have also divided the student. Each of us has a professional hold on our small part, leaving no one to deal with the student as a whole. Let's examine several examples.

Mr. Johnson, the truant officer, receives a referral to check on James Fagan, who has been absent for a week. He arrives at the Fagan home and Mrs. Fagan explains that James has severe bronchitis and should be back in school the following Monday. Since Mr. Johnson is there, Mrs. Fagan, who has had minimal contact with the school, asks how James is doing academically. Has he brought up his reading level? Mr. Johnson has to apologize as he explains that he knows nothing of James's reading level. He's "just the truant officer."

Martha is planning her schedule for her senior year with Ms. Oldmun, the guidance counselor. Martha would really like to take advanced senior math, as math is one of her favorite subjects. She thinks it may help her toward her vocational goals. Ms. Oldmun, having read the math teacher's recommendation, discourages the choice as inappropriate. Martha would like specific reasons as to why the choice would be inappropriate. Ms. Oldmun can give no specifics. She just has the sheet from the math teacher marked "inappropriate."

Mr. Bennett is a superior French teacher. In fact, he is so good he is the master teacher in languages for the system after hours. While talking with a colleague in the teacher's room during his prep period, he describes his problem earlier that day with Charles. He had come to class ill prepared, and Mr. Bennett had sent him to the V.P. When asked why he didn't handle the problem himself, he replied, "I'm the French teacher, not the disciplinarian. Besides, I have twenty-nine other students who want to learn."

In education today, we feel that specialists have a better handle on specific situations than do the generalists. Not true! Regular classroom teachers have the same skills as most of the specialists. They just need the support and confidence to use them. Special education is an excellent example. Nowadays when a teacher encounters a learning disabled (LD) student with special needs, the first response is to transfer him or her to an "LD teacher." What the regular teacher fails to realize is that the LD teacher has no magic bag of tricks. She or he may have some special skills, but LD teachers have nothing the regular teacher does not already have in some form in the classroom. The advantage most special education teachers have is a smaller class size in which to teach students who require greater teacher attention. I hate to burst the bubble, but a good regular teacher has most of the skills of a special education teacher. If you don't believe it, take a special education course! The role of specialist is important, but more as a resource to staff than in direct services to students.

THE BLAME'S ON US

Imagine this scenario: Dr. Hill enters Jack's hospital room and says: "Damn it, Jack, why the hell did you go out and get prostate cancer? Don't you want to live? Now I'm going to have to operate, and I'll have to postpone my golf game, thanks to you!" Ridiculous? Of course! But it is no more ridiculous than this example.

Miss Pacheco is working with Jackie in math. He continues to reverse his 5s on the paper. "Oh goodness, Jackie, why do you keep writing your fives like twos? Don't you ever want to do your math right? Now I'm going to have to sit with you while you redo this paper. I'll miss my free period thanks to you!"

We must stop blaming our students for their educational failures. Every time a student fails in our class, *we have failed as a teacher*. Obviously, we are not perfect and must accept some failure as normal. We cannot be all things to all people. We will not have a 100 percent success rate. But it is no more appropriate for us to blame a student for his educational problems than it is for the doctor to blame the patient for an unpreventable illness.

CHAPTER 3

System Thoughts

DECLINE IN DISCIPLINE—IT'S THE V.P.'S FAULT

In today's schools, the vice principal or principal has taken over most disciplinary responsibilities, leaving the teachers to teach their subject areas. While this sounds good, the whole idea is flawed. Good discipline is the basis for every classroom. You can be the greatest, most enlightened physics teacher in the world. But if you can't scrape the kids off the walls, your expertise will fall on inattentive ears and your efforts will be wasted. Every teacher's first and foremost task is to create an environment where learning can take place. This requires a standard of discipline and a plan for classroom management as the foundation upon which the rest of the classroom activities are built.

To rely on outside authority to establish discipline in your classroom is dysfunctional. Imagine parents' feelings if neighbors had to call the police because their child was beyond control in their home. Your first reaction would be one of horror. "My goodness, they had to call the police into their home to discipline their child! They've lost it!"

It's no different in school. If you must call upon outside authority to establish discipline within your classroom, you are telling the students that you do not have appropriate authority and control. This admission can lead to an even greater breakdown in your classroom authority. Obviously, there are times when you must involve the principal because of the nature of the problem. But these times must be narrowly restricted, as they will create future problems in your authority relationship.

SUSPENSION: WHO'S PUNISHING WHOM?

We spend thousands of teacher hours developing reading, math, and even sewing curricula. Yet even though we all realize that discipline is the basis of a good school program, most schools have spent no time in the development of a classroom or school behavior curriculum.

There was a time when suspension was a heavy punishment. Some years ago if a student was suspended the family would have been disgraced. The student would have spent the entire time at home under the mother's careful supervision. The student would have suffered. Today, more often than not, parents are not home to supervise suspension and it becomes a time for the "punished" student to get high and spend an enjoyable day with his girl, who has played hooky to help her cherished beau pass the time. What they do for the day is good material for the imagination and is certainly not punishment!

Suspension may be seen as good for the needs of the institution. It gets the misbehaving student out of our hair for a set time. But its effect on the student is probably minimal. In fact, for many students it can be rewarding. And we all know you don't punish with a reward. Even more ludicrous are school systems that punish truancy with suspension. Study that. It is wrong to miss school. As punishment you have to miss school. That's like punishing an alcoholic by making him or her take two drinks.

It is important that schools develop a behavior curriculum. Within it, they should define the stages of social growth and behaviors that are appropriate and a general expectation of the time frame for their mastery. Following that, they need to set appropriate interventions that can be used to recognize when a student meets the expectation, and others when the student does not. Careful attention must be given to reinforcements that are rewarding and to punishments that are punishing. Just because it appears rewarding or punishing to staff, don't assume that kids feel the same way. You may love mushrooms, but don't offer them to kids as a reward. At the same time it is important to develop the curriculum in such a way that classroom teachers can administer it without having to rely on the "disciplinarian" in the office.

CAPITAL PUNISHMENT IN TODAY'S SCHOOLS

It may sound funny, but we practice a form of capital punishment in today's schools. Of course we don't put students to death, but we brand them so that they carry the mark throughout their public school career. While we allow students some minor deviation in their experimentation with behaviors, extremes result in both appropriate and inappropriate authority reactions. The appropriate reaction, obviously, is punishment for the act designed to change behavior. The inappropriate reaction is the brand that never goes away.

In one instance, a thirteen-year-old male student made suggestive remarks to a female teacher while they were alone in the school elevator. The suggestion of sexual assault was made, though there was no overt act. School staff united over this serious act and demanded that the student be excluded from the school. The principal agreed and the exclusion took place. The student was permanently placed in a special alternative school for the remainder of his middle school experience.

Please do not misunderstand me. Such behavior is completely inappropriate and must be dealt with immediately using appropriate and significant punishment. But exclusion was not an appropriate punishment from which this student could learn from his mistake. He was not punished, he was banished. This is far too harsh a reaction to a onetime inappropriate behavior. Granted, were it to happen again, this might be a whole different situation requiring therapeutic intervention. But banishment for a onetime indiscretion from an emerging adolescent was the inappropriate ego reaction of a collective staff. Further, this incident went down in the student's file where it will be continually picked up in later school years.

Less extreme examples are found daily in many schools. Johnny hits a teacher. Granted, a bad deed. But one for which appropriate punishment is easy. But when he returns to school, assuming a suspension, staff points him out as that cretin who punched Miss Marigold, the reading consultant. Johnny senses the staff's feelings toward him and molds his behavior to meet their expectation. Rather than being allowed to learn from his mistake, that mistake sets the stage for his future behaviors.

Just as a student may learn math skills though initial errors, so too will a student learn appropriate social skills though a process of trial and error. While we must not accept inappropriate behaviors, we must understand that they can become an important part of the teaching/learning process of behavioral development and growth. This is even more important at the middle school level, when students find themselves exploring their new roles in a transition between child and adult.

THE "I HAVE TWENTY-NINE OTHER STUDENTS" COMPLEX

One of the greatest mistakes we make in the classroom is not dealing immediately with inappropriate behaviors. The easiest excuse is that there are twenty-nine other students in the class. "I'm sorry, but I am not going to waste time with George's misbehavior at the expense of the other students who are trying to learn." Out he goes. If that teacher had only realized that George has calculated that she would not take time to deal with his negative behavior. That was his planned risk. He came out a winner. Maybe he does not feel comfortable in the class because he is unsure of the material. To a kid it is much better to be *"bad"* than to be *"stupid."* But regardless of the reason, the teacher must deal with George.

The "other twenty-nine" is a cop out. Why? If you were to add up the collective time of George's disruption over the course of the year, he might be taking a total of several hours from the other students in the class. If the teacher were to stop the class now and deal with the behavior in five or ten minutes, she would probably resolve the problem so that it does not recur. Even if she has to repeat it two more times, she is still using only a small portion of the otherwise misused time.

At the same time, the teacher will be setting a behavioral example for the rest of the class. If George can get away with it and he is gone, what's to prevent Madge from pulling the same routine? It can become a vicious cycle unless controlled through immediate and appropriate interventions. Each classroom has unofficially assigned roles. When the "bad-ass" student is removed, the next in line emerges to assume that role.

THE RIGHTS ISSUE

In recent years, the issue of rights has been constantly before us. It began with the civil rights movement, progressed through women's rights, gay rights, and even is being talked about recently in regard to animal rights. Though I am a strong supporter of all rights movements, which give persons equal consideration regardless of their personal differences, we have all become so "rights conscious" that we have allowed our concern for rights to spill over into areas where they were never intended.

Children's rights are a good example. Beyond the basic human rights of warmth, food, health, physical safety, shelter, and a caring and nurturing environment, children do not have rights within a home. They do not have the right to privacy. Dad can open Johnny's bedroom door and enter without a warrant. They do not have the freedom of choice. Mom can require Johnny to be home at ten. And they do not have the right to democratic procedure. There need not be a vote to decide whether the family will vacation in the Poconos or the White Mountains. Yet, because of all the discussion of rights, children sometimes assume they have more rights than they do. Some parents feel guilty and "undemocratic" if they don't accede to these assumptions.

The same is true in regard to student's rights. All students have basic human rights. You must provide a safe environment. It must be warm, well lit, and dry. Students must have reasonable access to a drinking fountain, toilet, and lunch. They must also be free of arbitrary or prejudicial actions. But they do not have the freedom to come and go as they please; they do not have the right to go to the bathroom "right now!"; they have no right to vote on the rules of the institution; they have no right to rise and speak at will. In short, their rights are limited. Yet, how often do we hear the student's refrain, "You have no right to . . ."?

Schools are not democracies! As a school staff, we need not feel guilty about this. Each of our students has basic inalienable human rights and a right to due process. But this does not mean, as found by the Supreme Court, that each has the full civil rights of adults. Certain rights stop at the schoolhouse door when they become disruptive to the educational process. Even teachers have restrictions placed on their freedom of expression within their classroom.

GO TEAM!

The single teacher in the one-room schoolhouse had to rely on his or her own abilities as he or she functioned alone within the school environment. This privacy had some advantages, but it had far more drawbacks. Today's teachers have a decided advantage since they work within an environment shared by many other professional and support staff. Properly benefiting from this advantage, however, requires teamwork.

In this age of specialization, education has not escaped institutional divisions of labor. Where once there was the teacher, there now exists a guidance counselor, social worker, attendance worker, administrator, lunchroom aid, gym assistant . . . the list goes on and on. And this does not even mention the divisions within teaching itself—the math teacher, the English teacher, the fourth-grade teacher, the sixth-grade teacher, the art teacher, and so forth.

Given such specialization, it is important that school staff work together as a team. We cannot cut a student into many parts, with each specialist addressing his or her own piece. Such division presents fragmented services to the student with the sum becoming less than its parts. While the guidance counselor may work with a student to address a specific regrouping need, he or she must do so in conjunction with members of the teaching staff. Likewise, while the social worker may

attempt to resolve a home problem, it must be done in conjunction with staff members who deal with the student on a daily basis. Such coordinated effort leads to far more effective results.

In addition to benefiting the student, teamwork is also important for staff. When you as the teacher are having a bad day, it is good to know that other colleagues are experiencing it as well. We often personalize a problem day, failing to realize that everyone is facing the same situation. It's not you. The barometer or some other factor is affecting everyone. Unless you discuss this with those around you, it is easy to feel that it is "you," and such negative perceptions are a sure route to "burn-out."

Another important reason for school teaming is support. In dealing with a severe discipline problem, it is important to know that you have collegial backup within the sound of your voice. In such a way, you can remain confident in dealing with a very disruptive student who could turn on you at any moment. Besides giving you added confidence, this support makes students quickly realize that when they confront a member of the school staff, they are confronting a team. Such teamwork quickly diminishes a student's odds and is often effective in controlling a situation in and of itself.

Education is a team process. Unless you are taking full advantage of the strengths of the team, you are not benefiting from a resource close at hand.

CHAPTER 4

People Thoughts

PEOPLE ARE PART ANIMAL—A BIG PART

We have traditionally been taught to think that there is a major difference between human beings and animals. While human beings have characteristics that go beyond "animal," we are beginning to realize that the similarities are much greater than the differences. Both eat, drink, eliminate, sleep, and reproduce. Explain to me the basic difference between my building a fence around my yard and the dog who "lifts his leg" at the extremes of his territory. The underlying principle is the same.

PBS aired a series that surveyed the human mind. In one segment, the narrator stated that human beings and chimpanzees share over 90 percent of the same chromosomes. On first thought it seems a rather dramatic statement. The more one thinks about it, however, the less of a surprise it is.

One can see violent behavior as "animal" and develop a philosophy for dealing with the violent/acting-out student based on this perception. Interestingly, the Gorilla Institute in Woodside, California, looks at the converse. They are looking at the human qualities of gorillas. For many years, they have been working with Koko, a gorilla to whom they have taught over five hundred signs for sign language. They can "talk" with her. During their work with her, the trainers experienced a very interesting episode. Koko requested and was given a kitten, and cared for it a great deal. It was Koko's pet cat. Unfortunately, the cat was hit by a car and killed. Koko's trainer had the sad task of telling Koko, in sign language, that her cat had been killed. Koko "cried," gorilla style.

Rather than being opposites, human and animal behaviors occupy a continuum. At the lower end is what we call animal behavior. At the higher end is human behavior. (It could be the other way around, but I'll allow us to feel superior.) Just as Koko demonstrated higher-level behaviors upon learning of the death of her cat, so too do humans dip to lower levels when they exhibit violent behavior.

Animal behaviors are changed through training, not counseling, as can be seen in the following example.

Mrs. Smith returns home after an evening at the theater to find that her dog, Muftie, had left a large pile of "no-no" on her valued Persian rug. Mrs. Smith calls Muftie over to sit beside her and in a calm tone says: "Now Muftie, I am really hurt. I left you alone tonight for the first time in over a month so I could go to the theater with friends." Muftie wags her tail. "And look at what you left on my beau-u-u-tiful Persian rug." Muftie wags her tail again and licks Mrs. Smith's hand. "Now I will have to send it out to a special cleaners, and God knows what it will cost . . ."

At the rate Mrs. Smith is going, she can be guaranteed a pile every time she goes out. What she should have done, as any good dog trainer would tell you, was take Muftie to the pile, let her smell it, and in a very negative and loud voice say "BAD DOG!" Perhaps a little swat at the same time would be an extra good measure. Then, Mufti goes outside.

Instead, Mrs. Smith turned what she felt was punishment into a counseling session that reinforced Muftie's inappropriate behavior. The dog got attention and was spoken to in a calm, reassuring voice. The end result was rewarding rather than punishing. Consequently, the behavior will continue and probably increase in frequency.

The same thing is true when we deal with behaviors in the classroom. I am not opposed to sitting and discussing a particular behavioral problem with a usually well-behaved student. But for those students who exhibit continual behavioral problems, I am suggesting that we had best reexamine our approach as we are probably rewarding the behavior. Let's look at another example.

George has, once again, left the play area in a mess. You call him to your desk to discuss the problem. Poor George, he can't seem to do anything right. "Now George, I am really hurt. I left you alone in the play area so that I could work with some other students." George looks at Mary, and smiles. "And look at what you did in the play area. It's a mess." George nods at Harold and smiles at Mrs. Smith. "Now I will have to spend my whole free period helping you straighten up the mess."

The end result? George has gotten Mrs. Smith's undivided attention. Better yet, he will also get her sole attention during her free period. In addition, Mary knows that George is important and Harold did not get Mrs. Smith's attention during this whole process. George's nod said, "See who's in the spotlight now."

THE SHIFTING LOCUS OF CONTROL

Somewhere between kindergarten and the senior year in high school, an important classroom locus of control shifts from the teacher to peers. In elementary school, teachers' comments and praise are valued. During some period in the later elementary/early secondary years that locus changes. The opinion of peers supplants that of teacher as the more important.

Given that change, it is important that we learn to adapt our communication patterns and our reinforcement plans taking this into account. While applauding Johnny and bringing him to the front of the class in recognition of his outstanding work may be very positive and rewarding in third grade, it may provide the "kiss of death" to the seventh-grader.

It might be more appropriate in later years to provide recognition on a more personal basis: a note on the test; calling the student aside after class. This does not obviate general classroom recognition, but requires that it be prepared and presented with greater thought. If the classroom bully "poohs" and "paahs" a student who receives special recognition, it might be interesting to find a way to recognize that same bully on the following day. A taste of one's own medicine is often a potent cure.

THE WORLD OF TOPSY-TURVY

Another interesting phenomenon occurs along with that locus change. What was "good" becomes "bad." In years past, the "baddest" girl in class was a negative reference to her habits and mores. Today, the "baddest" girl is the best.

The same turn-around can be found in the classroom. Many people think that gold stars are appropriate recognition for the elementary student who has done well. Yet these same people feel that stars will not accomplish the same purpose at the secondary level. Not so. Gold stars can be just as rewarding at the higher levels, though we may need to learn to correctly interpret student reactions.

Johnny has progressed to ninth grade. On an outstanding essay the teacher affixes a gold star. As papers are returned, Johnny notes the gold star and comments that it is "stupid." He then shows the "stupid star" to his girlfriend and then to his buddies. He takes it home to show Mom and Dad: "Look at the stupid star that the teacher put on my essay." To admit that he is proud of the star would go against the topsy-turvy mores of his peers. So it becomes "stupid." As teachers, we need to understand the significance and meaning of his vocabulary, from his perspective rather than from Webster's. If it really were stupid, he would not have shown it to anyone.

MANIPULATION: A FUNCTION OF INTELLIGENCE

Manipulative behavior is a function of intelligence. The smarter the student, the more sophisticated the manipulation; the slower the student, the less sophisticated. Further, the more intelligent students seem to exhibit a higher frequency of manipulative behavior. Perhaps this is because they can easily become bored and find manipulative behavior entertaining. Or it may be because they can be easily frustrated, and manipulations can be an escape from that frustration. This second instance is especially true if the student is intelligent but functions below expectations because of learning disabilities.

Educators who work within urban areas with significant drug concentrations find that many of the drug addicts they encounter are of superior intelligence. It appears that they are better able to recognize the inequities and problems surrounding them and, feeling helpless to change them, escape through the use of drugs.

Since manipulation is a function of intelligence and is learned starting at birth, high-intellect manipulators are a challenge for the classroom teacher. If the student has a higher IQ than you, he will probably often win in the manipulation game unless you structure your classroom to give yourself the edge.

THE USE OF VIOLENCE—A LEARNED BEHAVIOR

The use of violence as a manipulative tool is the trademark of the highly sophisticated, negative manipulator. Violent behavior is animal by nature, but its use in the manipulation of another person is a highly skilled art. One must call upon sufficient violence to intimidate the other player, while not calling on it so much that other factors come into play. Perhaps a very negative facial expression toward the teacher is the appropriate manipulative stimulus. An open swear word would result in one's being sent to the office, which, in this situation, might be an undesirable outcome for the student.

Violence, or the equally powerful threat of violence, is learned early in life. Many of our behaviors are a result of rewards and punishments. Consider this example.

Little Frankie is sitting in the living room at home. He has been agitated all afternoon and is fidgeting on the couch. "Mommy, can I go out and play?" "Not right now, Frankie, we're going to eat in half an hour and I don't want you late." This "no" is the last straw in Frankie's bad day and he slams his fist down on the coffee table in frustration. An ashtray, which was near the edge of the table, falls to the floor, breaking with a crash. "Oh damn it!" says Frankie's mother looking in from the kitchen, "You broke my Niagara Falls ashtray. Get out! Just get out!" Frankie runs outside.

Without realizing it, Frankie's mother has reinforced his negative behavior. He got to go outside by accidentally breaking an ashtray. It won't be long before Frankie, if he is intelligent, learns that negative behavior gets him what he wants. It may happen consciously, but more likely it will occur subconsciously. If this reinforcement of negative behaviors continues, Frankie will develop into an antisocial child. He wasn't born that way. He has learned it.

Earlier, reference was made to the threat of violence. Consider the history of violence in a program for violent students, where we might assume that violence is a normal behavior. The program, which served over one thousand students in a ten-year period, experienced only ten assaults during that period of time. One thousand of the most violent students in a large urban school system assaulted the school staff but ten times. Such low numbers are not something that would be expected, but that was the reality discovered. In attempting to explain this, it was concluded that much of the previous violent behavior exhibited by these students in mainstream schools was allowed to get out of hand because it intimidated school staff. In the specialized program, violence was not threatening. The threat of violence had lost its sting. When it loses its sting, it loses its ability to manipulate. The behavior, in turn, becomes less frequent and often disappears.

LEARNING: A FUNCTION OF EVOLUTION

Darwin's theory of evolution has merit. An extension of that theory is that learning has evolved as an integral part of the human experience. All of the species that didn't want to learn died. Consequently, when a teacher claims that a student does not want to learn, one of two things is happening. Either the student is a "throw back" to the cavemen that died off, or the teacher is misjudging the situation. The latter is more probable.

The "lazy" student who does not want to learn does not exist. There are unmotivated students. There are remedial students who have a hard time with the skills of learning. There are students whose teachers have set nonproductive expectations. But a "lazy" student? Once again, we blame the student for our inaccurate assessments or inappropriate teaching. The need to learn is part of our basic nature as a member of the human species. Learning to master the complex tasks of walking and talking demonstrates a child's ability to learn. When children fail to learn within the school environment, the onus falls on us. We are the professional educators who must produce.

SUCCESS IN SCHOOL—SOCIETY'S REPORT CARD

As adults, we have many things to look to in judging our success. Our job title, salary, club membership, spouse, and so on, all show our success. But for a child, the single judge of success in society is success in school. Certainly, there are some things, such as Little League, that give kids a feeling of societal success. But the majority of activities that produce the feeling of success are school related. Report cards, school plays, school sports, the school newspaper, and other school-sponsored activities give most students their major societal rating. Even activities not related to school often look to school achievement and success as a prerequisite for participation.

Consequently, a student who is having problems in school is judged inferior in our society. That can be a heavy burden to bear. It sets a child's negative societal self-concept, which then becomes a self-fulfilling prophecy.

TOUCH ME

For a variety of reasons, teachers have stopped touching students. Threats of lawsuits, concern for sexual misinterpretations, and society's general move away from the "touchie-feelie" generation, have all resulted in teachers who walk their classrooms like scientists in a clean room, not touching anything. The same has become true in medicine. The field of medicine is reinventing the importance of the "doctor's touch" as an important component in the art of healing.

An interesting study also reflects on the importance of touch. The setting was a diner, and all patrons were treated equally well by the waitress, who was a very friendly individual. The only difference in treatment between two randomly divided groups was that one group received their change by having it placed in a change tray. The other group had their change placed in their hand with a slight fingertip touch to their palms. An interviewer then stopped patrons as they left and asked questions about the waitress. Those who received the slight touch when receiving their change had a significantly better perception of the waitress. Touch made a difference.

If you think about it, it makes sense. The most intimate form of human communication is touch. Would you rather have your spouse say, "I love you" or tenderly massage the back of your neck? Both things can say I love you, but the touch is a more meaningful form of communication (and less susceptible to manipulation).

In school, it is important to use touch on a regular basis. Touch is one of the most important factors in developing and maintaining rapport with students. As we walk around the classroom, we pause and examine the students' work. As we do so, we can place our hand on his or her shoulder, or lightly press our hip against him or her. There are many ways to touch. The importance is the contact, not its form. Some students respond to initial touch negatively, so it must be subtle. At other times is can be more overt. There is nothing wrong with a male teacher giving an adolescent female student a big hug when the student does an exquisite job in class. The emotion, however, must be real. Try it in your class. Positively touch each student every day for a week and note the difference.

Caution: There are obvious bounds that we, as professionals, cannot cross. While touch is important, it should not include private parts, nor should it be suggestive. We must use our common sense.

CHAPTER 5

Behavioral Thoughts

HYPERACTIVITY: THE GREAT AMERICAN HOAX

Education is a profession that continually places blame for professional failure on its clients. It appears that any child who deviates from "normal" becomes a candidate for some type of educational label. These labels, in turn, become an explanation for the lack of educational progress—thus excusing the teacher from responsibility. "I can't teach Johnny—he's LD." As with other educational fads, the label of the moment seems to change with time. At first it was learning disability, then hyperactivity, then attention deficit disorder, and now hyperactive/attention deficit disorder. While such disabilities do in fact exist, they have been greatly overidentified. A student who occasionally reverses a 5 to a 3 is not necessarily dyslexic. Johnny's inability to stay quiet in his seat is not always hyperactivity or attention deficit disorder.

True hyperactivity is a physiological condition wherein the body experiences a chemical imbalance. It is typified by "continual motion" behavior and the inability to remain on task. Over ten years of operation, only five of the one thousand students served by Hartford's Special Education Learning Center were considered significantly hyperactive. That's one half of one percent (.5 percent) of an already select population. The percentage of truly hyperactive children in a regular school is even lower.

It appears that all it takes to label a child hyperactive is some behavior problems, a mother who has reached the end of her patience, and an "understanding" physician. With the label comes unfortunate medication, educational excuses, and a sometimes screwed-up child. Obviously, this does not apply to that small percentage of truly hyperactive children who require such intervention. But it does apply to a large number of misdiagnosed children.

A student comes to a specialized therapeutic school with a history of several years of hyperactivity. He is on heavy doses of Ritalin, a drug that can have long-term negative effects, and spends most of the day walking around in a semi-comatose state. Because it is a therapeutic program dealing with behavioral change and the medication prevents it from effectuating such change, the school contacts the doctor and receives permission to withdraw Johnny from the medication.

School staff sit with Johnny and explained what they were going to do and why. They also explained the possible short-term effects he would experience while going "cold turkey." He understands that he might experience some behavioral problems during withdrawal. He also understands that while the staff cares a great deal about him, they still expect appropriate behaviors and will punish inappropriate ones. He accepts the plan.

What a week he had. His behaviors became progressively more violent and staff members had to punish him frequently. But by the end of the week, things calmed down and Johnny became a "regular" student. He was no longer a zombie and responded much more effectively to the behavioral programming. By the end of the academic year he had made enough progress to return to a mainstream school, where he functioned well. After six years in regular schools, he graduated from high school.

Why such confusion on hyperactivity? One of the reasons is that when we observe hyperactive type behaviors, we are too quick to jump to the label "hyperactive." It is important that we recognize hyperactive behaviors and attempt to determine their cause. When we do that, we will find that most often such behaviors come from something other than true physiological hyperactivity. Many of the hyperactive type behaviors are learned. Consequently, they can be unlearned, given appropriate structure and environment. Doctors now refer to this as situational hyperactivity.

Other cases of hyperactive type behavior come from nutritional imbalance. Such a student was Juan, who arrived at a school program with an extreme case of hyperactive type behavior. He was unable to attend to task for more than a minute. After careful evaluation, it was found that he was addicted to chocolate. This was the major contributing factor to his hyperactive behaviors. After the school got him off chocolate, he could stay on task for hours at a time. No miracle, just withdrawal from Snickers bars. If hyperactivity is a common diagnosis of behaviorally disordered students within your school, you ought to give this situation careful reexamination.

Some recent studies have found that diet changes behavior. Dr. Stephen Schoenthaler, reporting on a variety of international studies on the effects of diet, found that violent behavior in student populations could be reduced by up to 40 percent when students took a daily vitamin-mineral supplement. While educators are understandably weary of "simple fix-its," here is a collection of studies that seems to demonstrate a rather simple solution to almost half of a school's behavioral problems.

WHAT SKINNER'S BOX SAYS ABOUT GUM CHEWING

While educators all study some form of human psychology as they prepare to teach, most of these courses fail to apply the psychological principles taught to the classroom. Maslow's hierarchy of needs is important to the understanding of classroom reinforcements.

Likewise, all of us who have taken freshman psychology remember Skinner and his box. He placed a pigeon in the box and through trial and error it learned to push a lever. When the lever was pushed, a piece of food fell into the box and the pigeon ate. Each time the lever was pushed, another piece of food fell—one hundred pushes, one hundred pellets. Then Skinner began to mess with the pigeon. Food fell on every other push, then every third push, up to every thousandth push or so. As the frequency of return decreased, the pigeon pushed even harder and more furiously. From this came one of Skinner's basic principles of learning. Intermittent reinforcement is stronger than continual reinforcement. That is, getting the food once in a while is more reinforcing than getting it at every push.

We can see the same type of behavior at a slot machine. People stand in casinos for a long time, putting in money and pulling the lever, waiting for that once-in-a-while payoff. Or rub an instant lottery ticket—you know the feeling. You get excited when $10 worth of tickets wins you $2.

Although we have been exposed to this and many other psychological theories and principles, how many of them do we apply in our classroom? How many have taken an education course that teaches applied psychology for classroom teachers? Let's apply Skinner's box to the classroom.

Teacher's Perspective

It's Friday afternoon and payday. In ten minutes the final bell will ring and you want to get to the bank. It is then that you notice that Mary is chewing gum. Your standard classroom procedure for gum chewing is to have the student sit quietly in the punishment corner for ten minutes. But it's payday! You pretend that you did not see and go on with your end-of-day activities. The bell rings, class is dismissed, and you head for the bank.

Student's Perspective

You know gum chewing is wrong in class, but you love to chew gum. Besides, you don't always get caught. Uh-oh, she's looking right at me. I'm dead for sure. She's looking away and asking John to wipe the boards. Whew! I did it!

Without realizing it, the teacher has reinforced gum chewing with Mary. Partial reinforcement is stronger than continual reinforcement. Sometimes we can be our own worst enemy. Remember Skinner's box!

IGNORE BEHAVIOR—INVITE DISASTER

There are two schools of thought in regard to dealing with manipulative behavior. One teaches that if you ignore behavior it will go away. The second states that ignoring behavior will reinforce and/or escalate it. Experience shows the latter to be true. Perhaps you can ignore some mildly inappropriate onetime behavior when dealing with a very good student who is always well behaved. When dealing with a student with significant behavioral problems, however, ignoring inappropriate behavior invites disaster.

In general, ignoring inappropriate behavior creates two problems. First, by ignoring the behavior you run the risk of reinforcing it. Johnny says a bad word, but you choose to ignore it. Other students hear it and laugh quietly. The reactions of the other students reinforce Johnny's swearing behavior and its frequency increases. Now he swears more often to get the same rewards. Disaster one, and it's your fault. In addition, this attention-getting mechanism is modeled for other students who, in turn, may adopt it for the same effect.

Second, if he is looking for your attention or has some other agenda in mind and the swearing does not accomplish that agenda, he will escalate to the next step. Now he hits the student next to him and he gets your attention. Disaster two, and it's also your fault.

It is extremely important that you take the time to deal with each inappropriate behavior as it happens. You must do this to stop the behavior from continuing to occur and to prevent escalation. It takes time, but it is time well spent. If Johnny causes a two-minute disruption, it may take ten minutes of your time to resolve the situation. But ten minutes of time now saves two minutes a day times one hundred days and that equals an hour and forty minutes of disruption throughout the entire semester. To do otherwise is to be pennywise and pound-foolish. Deal with the problem while it is still small. An ounce of prevention is truly worth a pound of cure.

LOVE ME, HOLD ME

All children want limits. Setting limits for them is an expression of love and caring and provides them with security within their environment. It says, "I care enough about you to set controls for you." Even more difficult children, who seem to be fighting the controls we have set, are really testing our resolve. The more that they resist the limits, the more they are asking that they be maintained. Sometimes they make it very difficult for us to show our love. But we must maintain the controls as part of this process. To do otherwise shows a child that he or she is not worth our effort to care.

Society has created certain rules and laws that govern our participation within it. Breaking the rules means alienation from other members of the society. Breaking the laws means forceful separation from society through imprisonment. It is important that limits be set so that children can properly integrate into our society. The teaching of these rules and values, once primarily the function of the home, has become more and more the role of the school. The teaching of societal norms and limits is basic and must take priority over other school responsibilities. What good is it to teach Jacob how to read and write if he spends the rest of his life in prison?

THE EXORCISM OF VIOLENT BEHAVIOR

People who have seen the movie *The Exorcist* will understand this next example. For those who did not, the movie had to do with a young girl who was possessed by the devil and a priest's attempt to exorcise the demon. As the priest began his ritual, the devil, through the little girl, produced a series of repulsive behaviors. The little girl made nasty reference to the priest's mother, spewed forth green vomit, abused herself with a crucifix, and caused things to fly across the room. Each of these behaviors occurred in series, with the next outdoing the preceding. As the ritual approached its conclusion and the point of exorcism was near, all of the behaviors occurred simultaneously. Quite a spectacle, to say the least.

What does all this have to do with behaviors in the classroom? While no one expects a teacher to engage in the ritual of exorcism in the classroom, similarities can be found in the escalation of inappropriate behaviors with the disruptive child. The following example can illustrate this phenomenon.

The student who has become a discipline problem has developed a series of negative behaviors. It may start with subtle disruptions and culminate with physical assault. Human beings, by nature, prefer the status quo. Consequently, the student with discipline problems will resist efforts to eliminate those behaviors. You will find his or her behaviors escalating in your classroom as you begin to extinguish them. When this happens, many people will misinterpret what is going on. They assume that no progress is being made because Johnny is "getting worse." What they fail to realize is that Johnny is escalating his behaviors to maintain the status quo. If you continue, the behaviors may temporarily worsen. But don't give up. Just as in *The Exorcist*, you will reach a point where you will win as the behaviors are extinguished. Let me give you a specific, though extreme, example.

Erin had demonstrated several years of significant violent/acting out behaviors. On his first day at a specialized therapeutic program designed to remediate violent behavior, he was in reading class less than fifteen minutes when he began to have problems. The teacher asked him to do an assignment, of which he was capable, and he began his process of behavioral escalation:

Stage 1—Procrastination   While not overtly refusing to do the work, he was making no progress.

Stage 2—Open Refusal   When the teacher focused on the lack of progress, he refused.

Stage 3—Indifference   When told he would have to go to time-out for refusal to work, he said, "I don't care" and walked to the time-out room.

Stage 4—Verbal Abuse   When asked to stand properly in the corner of the time-out room, he became verbally abusive, "F___ you, I'll stand any way I G__ D___ please."

Stage 5—Threats of Physical Violence   His mouth was cupped (a procedure to prevent verbal abuse), and he threatened the staff with bodily harm.

Stage 6—Physical Abuse (Assaultive)   He became assaultive and had to be restrained.

Stage 7—Physical Abuse (Repulsive)   He struggled until he realized that we would not release him. Staff continued their technique of calming and positive talk. While his mouth was still being held he proceeded to blow his nose all over the hand that was holding him. Eventually, he calmed down and stopped his attempts to speak, and his mouth was uncovered.

Stage 8—High-Level Manipulation   As a last gasp effort, he feigned a heart attack, which, we learned from previous placements, was his custom. He requested transport to a hospital. It was explained that staff would be happy to comply. But first he had to stand properly in the corner for his punishment time. Then he had to return to class and finish the reading assignment. After that staff would be happy to call an ambulance.

Stage 9—Acceptance   He paused for a minute, let out a long, drawn-out sigh and stood in the corner to start his time. The sigh was his critical statement. He had tried his entire repertoire and nothing worked. He slowly realized the hopelessness of his case and let go with one of those wonderful sighs of resignation. Parents know them well. It was over. The behavior was exorcised.

After doing his time, he returned to class and completed the assignment. Since the ordeal had taken so much time, his school day was over and he went home. The next day he arrived at school one-half hour early and had an excellent day. The next two days were the same.

While this example is extreme, and much more than you will find in a "normal" classroom, it is true and provides a dramatic illustration of the extremes to which behavior can be pushed when a dysfunctional student is seeking limits.

VIOLENCE CONTROL—BRAIN VS. BRAWN

It is often assumed that it requires physical intervention to control a student exhibiting violent behavior. Not so. A great deal of violent behavior can be controlled mentally. This goes back to our discussion of animal behaviors and can be seen when we examine really mean dogs. Every time someone walks near their property, they are out on the sidewalk barking nastily. Pity the person who passes and is afraid of dogs. As they walk by on the sidewalk, the dogs charge out amid great bravado and the person runs scared. The dogs pursue, taking a piece of his derriere. On the other hand, a person who does not show fear often finds a different scenario. As they come out barking, that person remains calm and assertive. The dogs maintain their distance, deferring to that person's authority. Why the difference? Animals sense fear and build their behaviors upon it. So does the animal instinct in humans.

A good school example can be found when a weak substitute teacher enters a strong classroom. "Good morning class, my name is Mr. Paternuevo and I will be your substitute today. Please sit down young man. *Pretty please.* Yes, Miss? No, not now. . . . Oh, alright." And on it goes. The students have not planned anything. It develops as they collectively sense the weakness. Like wolves around their prey, they pack and attack. And just as wolves, they do not need an appointed hierarchy or a plan of attack. The actions of one student feed into those of another until the substitute is defeated.

Teachers who are fearful of students or have problems with the authority role shouldn't be in the classroom. It's that simple. They can be taught reading curriculum and math techniques, but the fear that is part of their personality can't be removed, not short term, anyway, and that fear is quickly sensed by the students and used to dominate them and their classrooms.

With that in mind, let's look at the brain versus brawn issue. Harry is out of his seat. You ask him to sit down. He refuses, saying "No!" There is no need to rush over and push him into the chair. Just give him a full-concentration look, eye to eye, and say in a firm voice "*Harry*, (pause) *sit* (pause) *down*! (pause) *Now!*" A strong personality rarely fails.

In another instance, Martha is having a bad day and raises her fist to hit you. You don't need to grab her. Just give her the same look you gave Harry and say, "You will do no such thing. Put your fist down, *now. Sit down.*" Ninety-nine times in a hundred, that's all you'll need.

In analyzing these examples, it is important to note two things. First, the teacher set an expectation that the negative behavior would not take place. Second, the teacher maintained a firm authoritative role and demanded compliance. In almost all situations, that is all that is needed. Do not expect negative behavior and do not ask for compliance—expect (demand) it. That's the required mindset to maintain discipline in any classroom.

PASSIVE AGGRESSIVE OR VIOLENT—THE DIFFERENCE IS YOU

For a long time we thought that there were two general types of behaviorally disordered students: the passive aggressive and the violent. The passive aggressive withdrew or escaped when confronted with a problem and the violent acted out. After many years of working with a severely behaviorally disordered population, we have discovered that the distinction between the two is not as great as was once thought. Further, it is not an either/or. The determinant as to whether a student is passive aggressive or violent is often the environment rather than the student him- or herself.

When Raul gets frustrated and confused he puts his head down on the desk and closes his eyes. You ask him to put his head up and get no response. He does not even acknowledge your request. But if you walk over and gently lift his head, he may very well slug you.

Rose runs out of the room when she is upset. Try standing in the doorway as she attempts to get out and she'll knock you to the ground. Both behaviors are initially passive aggressive. But when you thwart or block them, they can rapidly turn violent.

In an opposite reaction, Mark has just had a violent episode and was restrained. After struggling for several minutes, he now becomes quiet. When his violence did not work, he became passive aggressive and withdrawn.

Although a student may show a preference for passive aggressive or violent behavior, the two types are not mutually exclusive. A student may go from one to the other, depending on conditions within his environment. The difference, often, is you.

THE AUTHORITY RELATIONSHIP: DON'T PASS IT OFF

As the teacher, you are the ultimate authority in your classroom. This does not mean that you are a black-booted, lock-stepped, and mean spirited dictator. The authority role can be found in a caring and soft-spoken adult who maintains a continual smile and positive approach to students. Classroom authority means arranging and maintaining control of the classroom so that it is a positive environment for the teaching/learning process.

In that role, it is important that you maintain that relationship with students in your classroom and school and not pass it off. Each time you pass a disciplinary situation to the vice principal or ignore a behavior because the student "is not yours," you have given up some authority that may never be regained. There may be times when you need assistance. But even when the assistance arrives, you must remain in charge of the situation. Let's examine several examples.

In a school where a teacher develops a proprietary relationship with students in his or her classroom, the unspoken rule is "don't mess with my students." That teacher interprets other staff intervention as criticism of his or her own abilities. This teacher takes on a "mother hen" role and carefully herds her chicks around all the other hens in the barnyard. Students, being very smart, quickly realize what is happening and turn it to their advantage. They subtly flaunt their behaviors before other staff members, knowing that "mother hen" is close by to protect them.

As a result, other staff members have little authority with them. "You aren't my teacher," and they play it to the hilt. This is extremely dysfunctional since it teaches students selective respect for adults. We want to teach them to respect all adults in the school. Don't back away from these students. Deal with them as you would any other student in your school. If their teacher has a problem with this, talk it out in the teachers' room.

In another school, an environment has developed in which all teachers are responsible for their own students. In some ways this is a continuation of the tradition of the one-room schoolhouse. Teachers seem to feel that all is well if their classroom is functioning well. Rather than being a school, they are a collection of twenty one-room schoolhouses. When a problem occurs in the hall, each teacher closes his or her door, feeling the primary task is to keep his or her students controlled. Meanwhile, a colleague is being assaulted in the hall. If you find yourself in such a school, break away from the status quo. Discuss it with other staff. Don't back off from dealing with any student who may be causing a problem. Students must learn to respect all adults in your school, in the same way they must be taught to respect all police officers, all foremen in the factory, and any other authority figure.

In a well-run school, students see all staff as equal authority figures. (Obviously, staff members recognize and respect the school hierarchy.)

When a teacher has a problem in the classroom, the principal responds, as would any other staff member. Upon arrival, he or she is just another adult—not the principal—and he or she follows the directions of the teacher. The principal asks the teacher what he or she wants done and the teacher directs the principal. In such a way, the teacher's authority is reinforced with the students. How many times do we see the highly intelligent manipulative student playing one adult against another? The principal arrives in a class while a student is having a serious problem. The student turns and says, "You better do something about her" (referring to the teacher). The principal, trying his or her best to help in the situation, defends the teacher. Already we see two errors. First, the principal has taken over, at least momentarily, for the teacher. Second, the principal has allowed the student to redirect the problem from him- or herself to the teacher. The initial problem was the student's refusal to sit down, so what does "something about her" have to do with it? It is extremely important that school staff work as a team. The team leader in each situation should be the primary adult involved—not by rank, but by reality.

MAKE THE PAUPER INTO A PRINCE

Clothing and grooming reflect how we perceive ourselves at the moment. Imagine yourself in a gown or a tux. You feel formal, elegant. Now imagine yourself in your favorite casual clothes. You feel relaxed, comfortable, and warm. Now imagine yourself in your "grubbies" after working in the garden or under a greasy car. You feel dirty, sticky, and uncomfortable. In all three examples, you feel as you dress. Kids are no different. They feel as they dress and conversely, they dress as they feel.

A student enters your room at the beginning of the day dressed as though he just came out of a pigpen. He is dirty, his clothes are dirty, and he smells. How do you suppose that child feels? What is his self-concept? Poor, to say the least. His personal hygiene and dress are a reflection of how he sees himself. Furthermore, that poor self-concept is reflected in poor behaviors. What can we do about it? We can send him to therapy for a year or two and chances are good that things will change. But there is an easier and far more rapid technique. Bathe him, wash his clothes, and put him back in the classroom. Then note the difference. Not only is he physically cleaner, but the cleanliness positively affects his behaviors. Why is this so? Just as grooming and dress are a direct reflection of feelings about oneself, so too do grooming and dress shape those same feelings. Think about it. Put on a gown and you feel like a princess. Put on a tux and you feel like a prince. More importantly, you act like royalty. Kids are no different.

THEN PUT HIM IN A PALACE

Just as dress is important to our self-concept, so is environment. The space we occupy has a strong influence on how we perceive ourselves and how we behave. Put a person in a palace and he or she will walk with a royal gait, standing tall and proud. Put him or her in a church and that person will remain respectful and reverent. Put a person in a rathskeller and he or she will be loud, fun loving, and carefree. The space one occupies affects that person's behavior. The same is true of students in school. The space they occupy is an important behavioral determinant.

How often do we find the need for a "special" class in school and then have to search for space? Invariably, the space that we find is the least desirable in the school. Were it more desirable, it would have been occupied. Usually, it is the room next to the boilers in the basement, that old cloak room that is remodeled to handle a class, or the portable in the far outback. It is second-class space, steerage for those who remember the old liners. And the kids that go into it feel and behave second class as well.

A specialized school for severely disruptive students originally opened in an old dilapidated building. Plaster was crumbling, walls were wildly painted in "third world" designs by the alternative school that had previously occupied the space, and rugs were badly raveled. Recognizing the unsafe condition of the building, staff began at once to search for a better location. The only location available was a self-contained MIA (multi-instructional open-space area) in a regular elementary school. While not the ideal space, it was the only option available. You do not, however, put a group of severely behavior-disordered students in an area without walls. The school system had to build modifications including walls, ceilings, and so forth. Because the old building was in such poor condition, not to mention the fire hazard, it was decided to move into the new facility before the walls were installed.

It was assumed that there would be major behavioral problems with the students due to the distractions and inconvenience as work went on around them. To staff's surprise, however, the students had no problems at all! Carpenters were installing walls at one point using a gun that shot nails into the concrete slab floor. The students did no more than bat an eye. In fact, behaviors improved even though there was a great deal of disruptive construction activity going on all around them. When staff began to analyze this unexpected improvement, they realized that it was due to the positive change in the environment. The students were now in a beautiful new building, with new carpeting, natural wood cathedral ceilings, and fresh paint. They were proud of their new environment and proud of themselves, and their behaviors reflected that pride. Physical surroundings can have an important effect on behavior.

INVITATION TO FAILURE—RSVP

Students with a negative self-concept do not believe you when you see positive things in them. They are bad and they know it. You just don't know them well enough. In fact, they will often try to disprove your positive expectations through negative behavior. It is also their way of testing the seriousness of your expectation. When you see positive in a negative child's self, you have set up competition. Either you are right and the child is good, or the child is right and he or she is bad. Since none of us can live with such dichotomies, the child will quickly set up a situation to prove you wrong.

It's the first day of school and you are giving your traditional first-day pep talk. You are telling the class what a good year you will spend together, discussing how much academic improvement each student will make, and reviewing some of the textbooks that will be used. Rachael, who is repeating the grade because of the very poor year she had with your friend who teaches down the hall, makes a wise remark and has the students around her laughing.

You were prepared for Rachael. You read her records, talked with your colleagues, and knew she would be a problem. You stop your presentation, look directly at Rachael, and say, "So you're off to your same old routine. I'm not going to put up with this like Mr. Jones did last year. The next time you get funny, you'll find yourself in the office. Is that clear?" "Yeah," says Rachael expectantly.

What happened? Rachael was listening to you say that each student would make academic progress and have a good year. That made her uncomfortable, because she knew she wouldn't. She's "dumb" and she has stayed back. You're not talking about her. Just to prove it, her unconscious calls up the old routines. And your response reinforces what she already knew. Without realizing it, you have continued Rachael down the road to failure.

Let's take the same situation with a different ending. Rachael makes a wise remark and has the students around her laughing. You look directly at Rachael, say "Rachael" firmly, and continue your presentation. You pass out copies of the textbook for the students to look over and when they each have one you go over to Rachael's desk and ask her to step out into the hall with you. "Every student in this class is going to have a good year and you are no exception. I know that you had some academic problems last year, but this is a new year and I am a new teacher. It is my job to see that you improve in reading and math and I will do my job. Your job is to try your hardest. Further, your job is to be a lady at all times in my classroom. Do you understand?" Rachael, looking dejected, says, "Yes." You gently place your hand under her chin, lift it upward so her eyes meet yours and say "Now let's see a smile and then we'll go back in there and get our work started, ok?" Rachael, looking a little puzzled, tries hard at a smile and says, "ok." "Come on, a better smile than that." A broad grin emerges and you reenter the room.

The difference between the two endings is your expectation and your ability to hold on to that expectation when faced with countering behavior. If you hold your ground, the behaviors will change. Give in and she's well on the road to failure.

JOHNNY IS SMARTER THAN MISS JONES

Teachers feel that they are the smartest people in the room. They are right in regard to content knowledge. But some confuse this knowledge of subject matter with basic intelligence. There is a difference. As a math teacher, you have the greatest knowledge of mathematics. But that does not make you the smartest person in the room. In fact, if you assume that the average teacher has an IQ of 120 (higher than the norm because he or she has graduated from college), an average classroom of thirty students has probably four students with a higher IQ than the teacher. If you don't believe me, put it on the bell curve.

Since manipulative behavior is a function of intelligence, there are on average four students in the classroom that can run circles around you, the teacher. If you rely strictly on your intelligence, four students will leave you looking foolish. It is important that you structure your classroom in such a way that you have an advantage, even with the smarter students. Design the rules in such a way that IQ is not the sole determinant in the battle of manipulation. If you rely on your being the adult and therefore more intelligent, you will lose.

An important component of this design is refraining from debate. When you ask a student to do something, do not debate the request. The fact that you have made the request is sufficient information for the student and you do not need to provide an explanation. Let me give you two scenarios to illustrate:

Teacher: Johnny, sit down.
Student: Why do I have to sit down, Mary isn't sitting down?
Teacher: Sit down.

Teacher: Johnny, sit down.
Student: Why do I have to sit down, Mary isn't sitting down?
Teacher: Mary isn't sitting down because I asked her to do something special.
Student: Why don't you ask me to do something?
Teacher: I haven't asked you to do something, because you are not sitting down.
Student: I'm sitting down now, ask me to do something special.

As you can see, there is no need for debate. It wastes time and, if the student is a good manipulator, it will get you into trouble. John Rosemond of Knight-Ridder newspapers writes a newspaper column for parents. In one, he said, "Generally, parents err on the side of too much explaining rather than too little. 'Because I said so' is a perfectly legitimate explanation." His advice to parents is equally applicable to teachers. Explanations should be brief and are quite often unnecessary. A perfectly acceptable answer to "Why?" is "Because I'm the teacher."

CHAPTER 6

Other Thoughts

THE DYSFUNCTIONAL PARENT: ANNIE SULLIVAN REVISITED

The subject of parents' rights is becoming increasingly complex. There was a time when parents had the right to bring their children up as they saw fit. If you did not approve of how parents raised their child, you looked the other way. It was none of your business. Parents raised their children as they wished.

Times have changed. In many states school staff are now legally required to report suspected cases of child abuse. Courts are holding parents more accountable for the upbringing of their children. A parent who encourages his or her child's illegal acts can be prosecuted for contributing to the delinquency of a minor.

As a society, we have the obligation to protect the sanctity of the family from unwarranted intervention. But we also have the obligation to ensure that each child has the opportunity for maximum human growth. This should be true even when the parent is dysfunctional. The state can intercede in cases of parental neglect or mistreatment. Likewise the school must exert itself to ensure that students learn appropriate behavior, regardless of the parents' wishes.

There may be a family in which stealing is an accepted behavior, but the school cannot accept this. Though Mamie's parents and older siblings all have extensive police records, she cannot be allowed these same behaviors within the school. Schools must inculcate acceptable social values in all its students.

The movie *The Miracle Worker* is an excellent example of what happens when a teacher/parent conflict develops. It is the story of Helen

Keller, who was both deaf and blind. Annie Sullivan was hired to teach this educationally challenging student. She quickly recognized that the actions of Helen's parents were preventing her development. She saw through Helen's manipulations and realized that she would never learn as long as her handicap was used to excuse her poor progress and slow growth. Sullivan realized that the actions of Helen's parents had become dysfunctional to her learning and she gave them a choice. Either the parents allowed her to teach Helen without interference, or she would resign. Reluctantly the parents allowed her to continue on her terms. She and Helen moved into the rear house where their intensive educational program was uninterrupted. In a short time, Helen made the connection between feeling water rushing through her hand from the pump and the finger spelling "w-a-t-e-r." Her education had begun!

This movie is significant for educators. It teaches us an important lesson. If we really care about our students, there may be times when we must exercise our best professional judgment by standing up to parents and saying "no." Any less would not fulfill our responsibilities as teachers. Unfortunately, public school educators often reach that point and pull back. They fear confrontation with parents. We must strongly advocate on behalf of our students, laying the realities of their educational need before their parents. We must be Annie Sullivan to all of our students.

THE BEHAVIORALLY DISORDERED CHILD—A MANDATE TO TREAT

Just as we would not suspend blind and deaf Helen Keller because she could not hear or see, we should not suspend Alex, who is behaviorally disordered, when he misbehaves. All handicapped children have the right to a public school education, including those with behavioral disorders. We have the responsibility for developing an appropriate educational program regardless of the handicapping condition.

Yet we continually suspend the behaviorally disordered child, blaming him for his disability. "Alex, why did you do that?" is a common refrain. This is just as inappropriate as saying to the blind child, "Helen, why didn't you copy this as I had it on the board?"

As teachers we have the obligation to remediate each student's handicapping condition to the best of our ability. We must remember that behavior disorder is a handicapping condition and treat it as such. After identifying it, we must provide appropriate intervention strategies and remediation. You don't send the kid with a limp to the vice principal for walking funny. Neither should you send the behaviorally disordered child to the principal for his or her normal behavioral problems. We must stop blaming the behaviorally disordered student for improper behaviors and address the handicapping condition.

EMOTIONALLY DISTURBED CHILD—A CONFLICT IN TERMS

Since its inception, the Special Education Learning Center (SELC) has served over one thousand students. Almost all of these students entered our school with the label "emotionally disturbed." Of that one thousand, no more than twenty were truly emotionally disturbed—a modest 2 percent. Why are so many of our students mislabeled? There are three reasons.

First, in order to be given special education services, a student must be designated in a category of need. In Connecticut, school personnel have the choice of placing students with severe behavioral problems in one of two categories. The first is socially/emotionally maladjusted (SEM)—I suppose that is one who does not behave like a typical white, middle-class child. The second is emotionally disturbed (ED). Although a task force recommended it several years ago, Connecticut still does not recognize the category of behaviorally disordered (BD), though this is the most accurate label for a student with significant behavioral problems. Consequently, many students are labeled ED for lack of more appropriate categories.

Second, as educators we are continually looking at students to explain our failures. A student who does not learn must be learning disabled (LD), just as a student who does not behave properly must be ED. Teachers are quick to attach the ED label to the continually disruptive student because that immediately lets the teacher off the hook. As an example, Mr. Bates is having another problem with Hal. Miss Hinton, a teacher from across the hall, enters at that moment and is surprised at the behaviors that Mr. Bates is allowing. Her quizzical look draws Mr. Bates defensive response: "He's ED and we're waiting for testing and placement. You know how long that takes." Miss Hinton, understanding the emotions, frustrations, and personal admissions behind that short statement, responds with the all-knowing, "Yeah."

Third, ED is more appropriately an adult label and does not apply as well to children. Children go through many developmental stages as they mature. Much of their learning is by trial and error. Although children can exhibit a behavior that might be very normal for them developmentally, that same behavior in an adult would be abnormal. A little boy might fondle himself in public and it passes as a developmental stage. Let a company president do the same thing and he is labeled disturbed. Little Mary likes to hang from the swing upside down and yell "Geronimo." Let little Mary's mother do the same thing and they'd cart her off in a straitjacket.

There are some children who are truly emotionally disturbed, but the label is badly misused. The damage done by the misuse of the label overcomes many benefits the few truly disturbed might derive from it. Its use should be sharply limited.

CARING AND PERMISSIVE—ANOTHER CONFLICT IN TERMS

We must be careful not to confuse caring with permissiveness. You can care for a student a great deal without allowing unacceptable behaviors. Kids are great at attempting to confuse the two through guilt. Mothers and fathers know the routine. Teachers must be sensitive to it as well. In your class you do not allow a child to do something. She retorts, "You don't care about me. Mary can do it, because her teacher cares about her!" In her game, she confuses caring with permissiveness. Your response: "You can't do it because I care about you."

Because you care so much about a student, you will not let him or her do something harmful. Sometimes the harm may not show immediately and the child has a hard time understanding that. In school, limits are set. When an explanation is in order, it can be provided. A stock phrase, in response to their question "Why?," would be that it would be much easier for staff members to turn away and let them do as they wish. It requires much more work on our part to say "no." But we care about them and it would be incorrect to allow them to do what we think is wrong. Because we care, we are willing to invest the time and energy to say "no." While they protest it, they also appreciate it.

YOU ARE WHAT YOU EAT

Many articles have been published on diet and its effects on behavior. While the debate continues, educators have become firm believers in these effects. We are what we eat. This connection is especially true of the students with hyperactive type behavior. While the latest studies indicate that junk food, in and of itself, does not contribute to dysfunctional behavior, it has an important secondary effect. When a student eats junk food, he or she is not getting proper nutrients. And this lack of proper nutrients leads to behavioral problems. Give them a little sugar and they are bouncing off the walls. It seems that their idea of breakfast is a bag of chips, a bottle of soda, and a candy bar. Then they wonder why they are having concentration and behavior problems in class. It's like having a six-pack of beer and wondering why you have a slight "buzz." It is important to spend time explaining to students the importance of good nutrition and the possible effects of junk food and sugars on their ability to function in school. They work on it, but it's a difficult psychological addiction.

Because of the effect of diet on behaviors, it is important to pay close attention to ingestion of sweets during the school day. It is best to eliminate gum, candy, and other foodstuffs—even cough drops. The only thing allowed by mouth is the occasional sip of water from the water cooler and the school lunch. Sweets should be considered contraband and confiscated and destroyed. When students possess some, it's just a matter of time until they find their way into their mouths.

There are two other important points to be considered. First, the same rule applies for staff. We are role models. How can we say that sweets are bad for the students while we jaw on a mouthful ourselves? Being a role model is an important and demanding task.

Second, no junk food should be sold anywhere in the school. Many schools today see the sale of junk food in vending machines and the cafeteria as an important moneymaker. They might as well put rolling papers and cigarettes in the same machine. It makes about as much sense.

Student diet is an important area that schools must address. It is even more important for students with behavioral problems, since many of their problems are aggravated by what they eat. In the previous chapter I referred to the studies by Stephen Schoenthaler on the effects of daily vitamins and minerals in reducing violent behavior. It is time to apply these studies within the school environment.

TEACHING SANDBOX SKILLS IN HIGH SCHOOL

Most schools have remedial programs in academic areas for students who are behind in math or reading. Yet few schools have remedial programs for students who are behind in the development of social and behavioral skills. Though we all understand that appropriate behavior and social skills are important to a child's education, few schools have addressed the need for remedial programming for those students who have failed to master these skills. The standard response at the elementary level, in the few systems that have addressed the issue, is retention. If they don't pick up social skills, keep them back. Is that the answer? We don't retain for low math or reading proficiency. We provide remediation. Why should social and behavioral skills be treated differently? At the secondary level, such deficits are generally ignored.

Most students learn to share in the kindergarten sandbox. One has the shovel, the other the pail. "I'll let you use my shovel to fill your pail. Then, when you're done, let me use them both, ok?" Thus starts

the social skills curriculum. What do we do when a student has gotten to the high school level without developing these important skills? Present response is to ignore it. But that is as realistic as ignoring the non-reader. If anything, this student needs intensive remediation. This does not call for the installation of sandboxes in high schools. But the problem must be addressed with realistic activities for that age level. To say that the level for acquisition of that skill has passed, thus we cannot teach it, is doing a disservice to the student and creating a future problem. Remember, school is the primary socializing institution in our society. That role remains critical.

THE ONE-ROOM SCHOOL HOUSE, CONTINUED

One tradition in elementary education, which goes against common sense, is the self-contained classroom. It is defended because "younger children can't adjust to different teachers." In reality, it doesn't make any sense. Think about it for a minute, putting your traditional bias aside. You may try to rationalize the answer, but the fact is that we have them as an extension of the one-room schoolhouse.

There are many educational reasons to move away from the self-contained elementary classroom. If some structure is desired, students can be grouped using some criteria, by reading level for example, and rotated together from teacher to teacher. This allows for teachers to specialize in their area of expertise, giving all students the best in each area. The reading teacher is an expert in reading and loves the subject area. The math teacher is gifted in teaching math, hates reading, and is in his glory teaching elementary math. The same is true for the language arts teacher and the science/social studies teacher. All are teaching in the areas that they know and like best. None have to teach the subjects in which they have always been weak and in which they lack interest.

A second plus is that the students get firsthand experience with different types of adult figures. They have both male and female teachers; they have white, black, and Hispanic teachers. Each teacher has a different personality style. Students learn to work under a very strict teacher and a very quiet teacher. In short, students learn to adapt to five very different personality types within a consistent system of rules and regulations, working as a team.

A third plus is the ability of students to change environments every forty-five minutes. Getting up and moving from class to class does wonderful things for elementary students. Just changing physical environments invigorates the spirit. It gives definite closure to each period that can be lacking in a self-contained room. Best of all, it gives those student experiencing problems a chance to start the day over with another teacher. Maurie has started his day on the wrong foot with Mr. Suarez in reading class. Although the incident has passed, negative feelings remain on both sides. Then the bell rings and presto! Maurie walks into a new room and starts fresh. Further, if Maurie is having a bad day the burden is shared among his teachers.

This change of environment is not limited to helping after a behavioral problem. Occasionally, we as teachers have a bad day. Mr. Suarez had a bad night and is in a terrible mood. Rather than one group of students having to put up with his mood for an entire day, each group of students takes its share.

Self-contained elementary classes exist as a perpetuation of educational tradition. While many traditions are important and should be maintained, this one needs to be reexamined. A rotating class schedule provides a better education for students.

HONESTY—THE BEST POLICY

As role models for our students, it is important that we maintain a high standard of honesty. It teaches an important value by example and it allows us to develop a closer relationship with the students. Much of what we teach in values is done by example. We can discuss good values with a class, but the real teaching comes as they observe us in our daily lives. If we say that timeliness is an important value and continue to arrive late for class, our example will cancel what we have said. When John does something you do not like, which makes you mad, admit it. When he says "Why are you mad with me?" don't respond, "I'm not mad with you." He knows you're mad. It's hard to hide that emotion. Lay it on the table and be honest with him. Teachers are human and have the right to human emotions. "Yes, John, I'm mad because you . . . and I find that behavior wrong. It makes me mad when you . . ." Note, you are mad *at his behavior*, not at *him*. This is easier for him to accept and for you to express. While such an emotion can be painful for John, it is an honest one. Further, your honesty is appreciated. When you say, "I'm not mad!!!" with steam coming from your ears, everyone knows otherwise. Your dishonesty, while being socially understandable, lessens your influence and effect.

Let's look at another common example. You are wandering around the room and pass Frances, who has been doing marginal work. In your attempt to find something positive, you give her a false compliment. You say, "Why Frances, isn't this nice." It isn't. You know it, and more important, Frances knows it. While she smiles at your kind words, it leaves her with an uncomfortable feeling. The work wasn't nice at all. It is important that your compliments are honest or they will have less value. If you look carefully, you can find something to honestly compliment in any student's work. But it is important to take the time to find the right thing.

The same is true for students with significant behavioral problems. They know they have a problem and they know that we know it, so why deny it? Rather than hiding their handicapping condition under a bushel basket, we must treat their behavioral problems in an open, noncondemnatory fashion. If a student is referred to a special class for students with behavioral problems and asks "Why am I here?," don't cover up with the educationese: "It was felt that this is the best program to meet your educational needs within a highly structured environment." It is better to put it right on the line, "Because of your poor behaviors in the regular classroom." The student knew the answer to the question before he or she asked it and appreciates your honesty over the long term. In fact, the honest representation of their problem behaviors without condemning them personally (which oftentimes is the custom) establishes a bond between you. Be honest with your students. Even though it may be painful in the short term, it will reap rewards in the long run.

PIZZA PLUS

It is often traumatic for a student when he or she is moved from a mainstream classroom into a more specialized classroom, designed to meet their specific educational needs. Such a self-contained classroom can have a negative connotation, especially at the secondary level, and requires a special approach.

When such a special classroom is created, it is important that its teachers and staff have an initial meeting with the students who are being assigned to the group. In the meeting the nature of the assigned students' disabilities is discussed. As part of the discussion, the problems these students have experienced in the regular classroom are explored. The group talks about the problem that the other teachers are having in providing the affected students with the best education and the special training that the teachers for this group had. Everything must be laid on the line in an honest dialogue, allowing the students to ask questions and receive honest answers.

Once the students are aware of the move and understand the reasons for it, staff must address the experience itself. Such a move has negative connotations that must be combated by pairing them with positive things. The first can be pizza. During the first three weeks of the class, have a pizza party for that group once a week. Why? Because they are a *special* group and they are getting *special* things. Take them on several short educational walking trips. It didn't cost us anything but gives them added attention. The end result will be to positively portray this group as something. When students ask members of the special group if they were in that "new class," the kids responded positively. "Yeah, and we get pizza and go on trips." The questioning quickly focused on positives, rather than being in that new "dumb class."

It is important when you start something different for a special population within your school that you pair the difference with something positive. Kids, as well as adults, tend to see differences as negative unless they are properly presented. It takes planning and time at the outset but pays tremendous dividends over the course of the change.

BRINGING PHYSICAL INTO PLAY

Although emphasis throughout this book is on verbal control of problem students, there comes a time when physical intervention is necessary. Before engaging in such activity, however, it is important that you carefully examine school and district policy, state law, and basic common sense.

In dealing effectively with a severely behavior-disordered student, the ability to use physical intervention is critical to success. This student has successfully used the threat of physical violence to manipulate their school environment. The only way such manipulative behavior can be brought to an end is by showing the students that it no longer generates fear and gets them what they want. This sometimes requires the use of physical restraint in the process.

Three important points require early clarification. First, physical restraint and control is neither corporal punishment nor offensive (as opposed to defensive) behavior. It is used in response to a student's actions to bring him or her under control. Second, physical restraint is rarely needed. Just knowing that it can be used is often enough to deescalate a situation. Third, physical control requires appropriate protocols and staff preparation.

While outside the school, you observe two students in a heated verbal exchange. You rush over, arriving as punches are about to be thrown. In a very authoritative manner, you step between the students and order them to stop. One student complies, but the other continues to threaten and attempts to strike the other. You grab the assaulting student in a bear hug as you call for assistance. Such action is not corporal punishment. In fact, it is not punishment at all. It is restraint. Further, it is the least amount of restraint required in the situation. Had you rushed over while the disagreement was still a verbal exchange and slammed one of the students to the ground, your actions would have been wrong. That would have been more physical intervention than was called for at that time in that situation. You must use only as much physical intervention as is necessary to control the situation. In fact, if you do not separate the students and one is seriously hurt, a case could be made for your negligence.

Physical intervention, when available for your use, is rarely needed. Students use verbal threats and manipulation because they know they have the upper hand. In an extreme situation, Johnny can insult your parentage in front of the entire class and when told to go to the office, suggest other sexual activities for you. What do you do? The principal arrives and Johnny suggests the same acts with you as the partner. Johnny has gotten the upper hand, knowing your limitations in the situation. Without the ability to physically remove him from the classroom, you have lost the battle.

When a school has the ability to use physical intervention, they rarely need it. When students know it is available, their behavioral outbursts can usually be verbally controlled.

CHAPTER 7

Classroom Techniques

DEVELOPING A BEHAVIOR CURRICULUM

As educators, we are familiar with curriculum. It drives each of our subject areas. It develops educational sequences and provides techniques and options in the presentation of subject matter. There is a major void in our curriculum system, however. Although student behavior is an important part of any classroom, few of us have a behavior curriculum for our classroom/school. One of the most important areas in our educational program does not have a planned sequence and system. If you do not have such a curriculum, however, you are not alone. Few of the country's experts on educational curriculum are aware of the existence of any such behavior curriculum.

In developing your classroom/school behavior curriculum, there are three important components that must be addressed. First, you must define the appropriate and inappropriate behaviors within your classroom/school. These are developed given the age and intellectual development of your students. The behavioral curriculum in a high school will obviously be more sophisticated than one at the elementary level. At the same time, there may be higher expectations for academic students when compared with slow learners.

Second, you must determine a system of positive recognition and negative consequences (rewards and punishments) appropriate to the students in your class/school. Although you will make the initial determination, make certain that the students perceive your rewards as positive and your punishments as negative. We may all love mushroom soup, but don't offer it to the average fourth-grader as a reward. Likewise, while

suspension was a severe punishment in our day, be careful it is not perceived as a time to watch television with a favorite beau today. Further,
recognition and consequences may have to be varied depending on the
student involved. Keeping most students after school for detention is
negative. But some students thrive on the extra attention.

Third, you must develop a management system that delivers the
recognitions and consequences. Consistency, immediacy, and in-
evitability are the basis for every system. These must be applied on a
regular and consistent basis to all of your students. The system must reward positive and punish negative behaviors as close to the behavior as
possible. And, as night follows day, students must understand that your
system's consequences will follow their actions. A behavior curriculum
is the important base for your classroom management plan. Spend
some time developing it, keeping the following components in mind.

IS YOUR CLASSROOM DESIGNED FOR DEFEAT?

When one builds a house, it is important to consult an architect who can
suggest proper kitchen layouts. There are important functional principles that are employed when designing the working space. The stove,
sink, and refrigerator all have to be placed within a certain spatial relationship to make the kitchen functional.

Although none of us would think of constructing a house without
some architectural assistance, we often approach classroom layout with
little regard to functional design. Traditionalists utilize equal rows
spaced equidistant across the classroom, with the teacher's desk front
center. Progressives have interest centers grouped around the room.
The rest of us are somewhere in between.

When arranging the classroom, examine the way classroom layout
affects classroom interaction. Arranging desks in circles instead of
rows, for example, encourages discussions. Studies have shown that
desk arrangement affects student behavior more than student ability or
interest.

Other important factors must also be taken into consideration. Since
a messy room provides a cue for a disorderly class, material storage and
furniture placement is important. Everything must have its place. Further, materials must be accessible if they are to be used.

Also important is the development of good traffic patterns. If student movement is important to your learning environment, is such movement easy? Can students get to the materials they need without disrupting others? Is there an easy flow as students move from their desks to an interest center? If your room has restricted areas that logjam during movement, expect students to pause and get off-task as they reach such areas.

Is the room size appropriate to the number of students? Just as too many students in a room can be detrimental, so can too few. All too often, school districts develop a new class for ten special education students and then place that class in a regular classroom designed for thirty. In walk the ten students, who proceed to position themselves all around the room. It's like church. No one wants to sit in the front rows. The teacher then has the never-ending task of moving the kids to the front.

A far easier strategy involves preventative design. Before students enter the room for the first time, all but ten student desks are removed. File cabinets, bookcases, and other pieces of classroom furniture are used to partition off a usable classroom space. It becomes manageable for the size of the class. Peripheral space can be used to develop special interest areas and for other purposes.

It is important that your classroom design complement and facilitate your instructional design and teaching style. Is your classroom designed for success or failure?

START THE DAY RIGHT

We are all creatures of habit. Students are no exception. It is very important that each day/class gets off to a good start utilizing a consistent routine. You need a commonly understood signal that lets the class know that the class is to begin. Perhaps it is your saying "Good morning, class," or flashing the lights off and on once. Or it could be subtler, such as your standing at the front of the class. Whatever the signal, the students realize that it is time to sit quietly in their seats while giving you their attention.

At the beginning of the day, open with an appropriate salutation and a group exercise such as the pledge of allegiance, a song, or your reading of the daily announcements. This gives the class a feeling of "group" as students participate together in the exercise. It also signals the day's beginning. No student can claim that he or she didn't know the day had begun.

Once the class has started, a common classroom routine is helpful. If a specific student has been given the responsibility of passing out paper, indicate this through a nod. Students should understand what is expected of them and get to work. "All right class, start your math— assignments are on the board" should be sufficient to begin the regular routine. "Give me your attention please. Today we are going to start a new activity" clues them to you for new instructions.

SETTING EXPECTATIONS

Once your classroom management plan is developed, you need to communicate it to your students. Traditionally, we associate a classroom management plan with rules. How many times do we walk into a classroom and see something similar to the following posted on the wall?

Rules of Miss Alcatraz's Room

1. **Don't** get out of your seat without permission.
2. **Don't** talk without first raising your hand.
3. **Don't** write in the books.
4. **Don't** forget your homework.
5. **Keep your hands to yourself!**
6. **Don't** copy other's work or cheat.
7. **Don't** touch the light switches.
8. **Don't** run and push in line.
9. **Don't** touch anything on my desk.
10. **No** gum, candy, or food.

Wow! What a first impression. A list such as this has several problems. First, its initial message creates a very negative environment. Just reading it leaves one with a very negative feeling. Welcome to prison! Second, the teacher has set negative expectations for student behavior that, in turn, invites them. The initial expectation is for inappropriate behavior. Third, it is educationally unsound. As educators we understand the importance of teaching from a correct example—2 plus 2 is 4, not 2 plus 2 isn't 3 or 5 or 8. Fourth, the list is too long. We understand from experience that any list of more that four or five items isn't read. And lastly, the smart student will rapidly find a negative behavior not covered by the list. "It doesn't say I can't sail paper airplanes!" So the next day there are 11, and then 12 until there isn't sufficient wall space for all of the "rules."

Rather than negatively phrased rules, try listing your classroom expectations. They must be stated in a positive way and should be general enough to cover all possible behaviors. Here's an example:

Welcome to Mr. Petty's Room

We are very proud of our classroom and welcome you. While you are with us you will find:

1. We behave ourselves as ladies and gentlemen.
2. We respect school property.
3. We respect each other.
4. We work very hard on our assignments.

In contrast to the first example, these expectations are positive, use a few general items, and create an expectation for positive behaviors.

Let's revisit the plane sailor as an example. "John, gentlemen don't sail paper planes in class. Please don't do it again." We interpret the specific behavior within the general code of conduct. Everything fits within these simple expectations and it makes classroom management much easier. There is no debate, since you are their official interpreter.

Once you have determined the expectations for your classroom, they must be communicated to the students. And this communication goes beyond the traditional "poster on the wall." Just as with any subject that must be mastered, expectations must be taught. This requires that the teacher dedicates classroom time to teach the expectations, including examples of appropriate and inappropriate responses to each. Behaving as a lady or gentleman may elicit different examples of day-to-day behavior in first grade as compared with seniors in high school.

Sufficient time at the start of the school year must be taken to present, review, and reinforce these expectations. Then, throughout the school year, the teacher can continue to reinforce this teaching as he or she recognizes and compliments students who have met an expectation through specific examples of classroom behavior or academic accomplishment.

EXPECTING SUCCESS

In chapter 1 we discussed the importance of setting positive expectations for students. It is important that such expectations are reinforced through appropriate classroom recognition. One such technique is simple, though often overlooked.

When correcting papers, give feedback to the student through the number correct rather than the number wrong. On a math quiz with twelve problems, nine correct focuses on the success of the student; three wrong focuses on failure. Although both results indicate the same performance, concentrating on the number correct gives positive feedback. It's like the old argument over whether a glass of water is half empty or half full. In the same way, we need to highlight the best grades on an assignment, rather than the worst. It is important that we set "good" as the class expectation and then focus on the best as we recognize achievement of that goal.

The same principle is true when setting behavioral expectations. Students tend to rise to our level of expectation, whether that expectation be academic or behavioral. An often-occurring negative example of this would be when, at the start of the school year, the teacher recognizes the last name of a student whose family is known for problems. "Mary Jones? Is Johnny Jones your brother? . . . Well I want you to know that I will not tolerate any of that foolishness in this class, young lady." The expectation is set and Mary, reacting to this negative introduction, begins an attitudinal change.

Many behavioral problems in the classroom are initiated by a teacher's inappropriate expectations. The teacher inadvertently sets a negative expectation for a student's behavior. The student, seeing the teacher as an important significant other, then responds with that behavior so as not to let that significant other down.

A classic example: "All right students, please line up for the cafeteria. Johnny, I hope that you can stay in line and keep your hands to yourself today. Johnny, *what did I say*? In line! Hands to yourself! You'll never change!" And he won't.

THOUGHTS ON REWARDS

When developing a reward system, one often begins with a focus on material rewards for good behavior. One will quickly discover, however, that the recognition of good behavior is more important to the student than the material rewards themselves.

Consequently, your reward system does not have to be elaborate. "Good job!" is a real plus. Gold stars and scratch-and-sniff stickers are a turn-on—even at the high school level. An instant snapshot of the "Student of the Week" on the bulletin board is almost heaven. A round of applause can do wonders.

Rewards do not always have to go to the best. You must also reward the student who tried the hardest, made the most improvement, or was the most creative in approaching the task. In such a way, rewards find their way around the room. It is important that each student be rewarded regularly.

At the same time, rewards must be honest. Don't give Johnny a star for a marginal paper just to recognize him. Starring marginal work lessens its meaning. Spend the time necessary to find something of Johnny's that merits recognition. There is nothing wrong with giving a star for a good cursive "a" in a high school class for severely LD students.

A point system, possibly rewarded by some material recognition, can also be effective. The next section presents several point systems. While awarding the points is in and of itself reinforcing, you can add to their importance by periodically doing something special for the students with the highest number of points. A VCR cartoon during recess, a piece of pizza at lunch, or a skating party are a few of many possibilities. Rewards are restricted only by your imagination.

Some caution needs to be given when developing a rewards system in middle and high school. As discussed in chapter 4, students during their elementary years see the teacher as the important significant other within the classroom. As they mature, the locus of importance shifts from the teacher to peers. Consequently, while teacher praise in elementary school is a great plus, it can become a negative from peers at higher grades. What might have been rewarded best in front of the class in third grade might better be done less publicly in ninth.

While we are focusing on recognizing the accomplishments of an individual student, group rewards can also be very effective as well. One very easy technique is using marbles and a glass. Each time someone in the class provides an excellent response to a question or demonstrates an outstanding behavior, the teacher drops a marble into a glass on their desk. When the glass is full, the entire class shares in a reward—for instance a video or snack treat. At the beginning of the year, start with a smaller glass and larger marbles. As the year progresses, the glass can become larger and the marbles smaller—a natural deescalation of the reward system. This is just one of many possible techniques in group reinforcement.

THOUGHTS ON PUNISHMENT

Students must see punishment as a negative event. It is important, therefore, that you carefully evaluate punishments to make sure that the affected student perceives it in that way. In earlier sections we discussed suspensions that have lost their sting and after school detentions that provide desired attention.

The most punishing thing a human being can endure is boredom. That is why solitary confinement is used in adult prisons for the most recalcitrant prisoners. Although I do not recommend solitary confinement for your classroom, there is a school-appropriate technique that employs the same principles. You can call it the "Quiet Corner," "Disney World," or any other name you like.

In your quiet corner, students who have exhibited inappropriate behaviors are punished. They must sit, facing the wall, hands folded on the desk, with nothing to do. It quickly becomes boring—the basis for the punishment. Unlike some other techniques, your quiet corner does not give the child work. Giving a student work to complete as punishment is incorrect for two reasons. First, the idea of this form of punishment is to create boredom. When given an assignment, no matter how trivial and repetitious, it provides the student with something to do. While writing one hundred times "I will not . . ." is perceived as punishing, the creative student can quickly turn it into a game: "I . . I . . . I . . . will . . . will . . . will . . ." And the game is better than doing nothing at all. Second, the use of academic work as punishment is sending the wrong message. If I am the math teacher, twenty-five additional problems in mathematics should not be given as punishment. Mathematics is fun and an important skill for the future—not punishment!

To prevent manipulation during time in the quiet corner, divide it from the rest of the room with a visual barrier like a file cabinet or bookcase. Arrange it in such a way that you can supervise the student, but other students cannot see the one being disciplined. Such a physical arrangement prevents the student from entertaining others without your realizing it. It still requires your close attention, but minimizes sneaky manipulations. Try it. It works!

Ten minutes in the quiet corner is quite effective. Do not feel that it has to be any longer for a minor infraction. Teachers often overreact by giving greater punishments than are necessary. This works to our disadvantage, since a thirty-minute punishment requires thirty minutes of our time as well. By going to the quiet corner the student has deferred to your authority. Goal one is accomplished. Time in the quiet corner is geometric in nature. The tenth minute is ten times more punishing than the first. After the first few minutes, the cuteness wears off and it becomes uncomfortable. Goal two is accomplished.

Don't let student claims concern you. "Ten minutes in the corner doesn't bother me." Not true. This comment is like a student's "Go ahead and call my mother. She won't care," as he prays silently that she will not be home. If it appears that ten minutes is really not effective with the student, make it twenty minutes. It may be effective to respond to the "Ten minutes doesn't bother me" statement with "Fine, make it twenty." But it should not escalate beyond that point.

Creativity is just as important for punishment as it is for rewards. The quiet corner is very effective, but you are free to use your creativity as well. A student lets the air out of a teacher's car tire. His punishment? Remove the spare tire from the car, get a hand pump, and let the student inflate it. When finished, let the air out and have him pump it up again. After a half-hour of this, he will learn the meaning of punishment. If you have ever hand-pumped a car tire you know the feeling. The punishment is good because it pairs the punishment with the crime.

A student is throwing spitballs. Have that student remain after class and give him or her paper with the instructions to make one hundred spitballs. When finished, have the student throw the spitballs, retrieve them, and throw them repeatedly until he or she never wants to see another spitball again. The psychological principle is simple. We have paired the undesirable behavior with an uncomfortable experience, thereby decreasing or eliminating that behavior.

VERBAL CONTRACTS

The verbal contract is an important tool in your classroom. Once students verbally agree to certain tasks or conditions, they are generally true to their word. Further, a verbal contract is quite simple to use and requires only a short period of your attention.

John continues to fidget and has yet to complete the first problem of ten assigned. You know he is capable of completing the assignment. This scenario follows:

Teacher: John, you have only completed the first problem. We have twenty minutes left in class, which should give you enough time to complete the assignment. Do you need some help?
Student: No, I know what to do.
Teacher: Fine. I expect you to complete the assignment by the end of the period. I know that you don't want to stay after school to complete it. Do you understand?
Student: Yes.

The contract has been set.

Verbal contracts are also valuable following a punitive action. Mary has sat in the quiet corner ten minutes for continually leaving her seat without permission. Her time is up and you approach her.

Teacher: Mary, your time is up. You may return to your desk if you are ready to remain seated and begin your work. Are you ready?
Mary nods her head affirmatively.

Teacher: I want to hear your answer. Are you ready to return to your seat, remain seated and do your work?

Mary: Yes.

Teacher: I know that you will have your work completed so that you will not have to stay in for recess. Do you understand?

Mary: Yes.

Teacher: Fine. Go back to your desk and begin work.

Verbal contracts have three important components. First, you must set out the specific behavior/task that you expect from the student. In John's case it was ten math problems. In Mary's it was remaining in her seat and doing her work. Even though her work was not spelled out in the contract, it is understood that she was aware of the specific assignment.

Second, there should be a consequence for failure to complete the contract. John would return after school to finish the work. Mary would miss recess. It is important, however, to phase the consequence in such a way that it does not present an expectation for failure.

Third, it is important that the student verbally acknowledge your conditions. A verbal response is clear, easily interpreted, and an indication of acquiescence to your expectations and conditions. Without a verbal agreement, the contract is incomplete.

Verbal contracts are also very helpful in ending disciplinary situations. If Mark has to be excluded from class following a disciplinary problem, a verbal contract is good before he returns. His agreement is a good indication that he is accepting your authority and the problem behavior is resolved. His refusal to agree indicates that he is not ready to return to class.

Mark was sent to sit in the office for repeated inappropriate language. At the end of his time, you go to the office and the following conversation takes place.

Teacher: All right, Mark. Your time is up and you may return to class. Before we go, however, I want to make sure that you understand that inappropriate language will not be tolerated in my class. Are you ready to return to class and keep your language appropriate?

Mark: *silence*

Teacher: Are you ready to return to class and keep your language appropriate?

Mark: *continued silence*

Teacher: Fine. You can remain here in the office. When you are ready to return to class on my conditions, have the secretary call me and I'll come back.

You return to class. Mark remains in the office until he is prepared to meet your conditions. If you do not get the call that day, he begins school the next day in the same situation. The only way he can return to your classroom is through acceptance of your verbal contract. Prolonged refusal may require another approach. This technique, however, generally works well.

GIVE NEW STUDENTS A FRESH START

When dealing with a new student, we must base our evaluation of that student on our own perceptions. Consequently, it is best to leave the written records on a new student unopened until such time as we have formed our own conclusions and opinions. This is even more critical with difficult students. It is important that we do not let others' negative impressions color our own judgments. When our judgments become colored, they can set a subtle set of expectations that will draw out the negative behavior in the student.

John arrives as a new student in your class, accompanied by his school records. In reviewing the records you find continual reference to his "laziness." You immediately perceive John as a lazy student and expect such behavior. You subconsciously lower your expectations for him, realizing that lazy students will not produce as much as regular students. John, sensing your lowered expectations, sees his new school start as "business as usual" and continues his old routine.

Mary arrives in your class with a history of poor reading skills. You note her second-grade reading level and assign appropriate work. What you fail to realize is that she, through some omission in her early schooling, failed to learn the names of ten of her letters. This left her reading far below her otherwise average abilities. Had you done your own informal testing, you would have noted that omission and could have rapidly filled the void.

Except for certain health conditions of which you should be aware, it is better to leave student records unread until you have formed your own opinion of each student. In such a way, you will not allow the opinions of others to subtly affect your judgment. This prevents the carry-over of errors and gives the student a truly fresh start in a new school environment.

REPORT CARDS NEVER COME

In elementary psychology, we learned that immediate rewards and punishments are very important in molding behavior. Yet, except for the grade on an occasional quiz or exam, the only official feedback that a kid often receives is the report card every three months. Kids need more immediate feedback. They can't postpone rewards for three months. In the same way, delayed punishment is less effective.

A very simple report card can be developed (Figure 7.1) which is done on a periodic basis. It is simple (complicated systems with a check for each fifteen seconds on task are compulsive and impossible to manage), quick, and easily understood. At the end of each classroom period the student can get one point for doing a full period of appropriate work and two points for a full period of appropriate behavior. In this particular example, emphasis is on behavior over academic ratio of 2:1. If the emphasis of your class is different, the system can be easily modified.

NAME _____ DATE _____					
PERIOD	1	2	3	4	5
BEHAVIOR					
ACADEMIC					
TOTAL					
Bathroom _____ TOTAL POINTS _____					

Figure 7.1   *Sample of Simple Daily Report*

At the end of the class, the teacher gives academic and behavioral points. Students can receive full, partial, or no points depending on their classroom activity as judged by the teacher. Points are not open to discussion. You may make a short explanation when appropriate. For someone who has done very well, it may be good to put in a few words of support and praise. For someone who has had a problem, you might verbalize the problem so that you are both on the same wavelength. This explanation is often unnecessary, however, and can be omitted. If Mary did all of her work appropriately and in good time, she gets her entire academic point. If she did not complete as much as she should have, or completed it in a less than acceptable manner, she might get one-half point. If her work was unacceptable, she gets no academic point. In the behavioral area, she gets all of her behavioral points if she had good behavior throughout the period. If she got out of her seat without permission, she might get only one and a half behavior points; if she had a verbal disagreement, maybe one point; and, if she had to be disciplined, no behavioral points at all.

There are two important things to keep in mind when giving points. First, give them honestly. Don't give points to be nice. Points are earned. Students can get them at different rates but they are earned, not given. Second, be sure to separate the academic from the behavior. In such a way, you can reinforce good behaviors while punishing poor academic performance and vice versa. When only one rating is given, you are forced to tie the two together, thus restricting your options.

Behavioral points can also be broken down into sub-areas (Figure 7.2). Rather than just "behavior," students are rated plus or minus in sub-areas. Additionally, there is a final category that can be developed individually by the teachers for each student. If Mark has a problem with staying in his seat, this might be his final category. If José has a problem with humming, that might be his. Each "+" then translates into one point, with the sub-areas adding up to a total of five behavioral points. Academic points total two and one-half so that we still maintain the 2:1 ratio.

These systems are excellent because they are simple to administer and give immediate feedback to the student on his or her progress. In effect, it is a report card after each class. There is no doubt in the student's mind as to how well he or she did. For the student trying to im-

NAME			DATE		
PERIOD	1	2	3	4	5
Ready to begin on time					
Follows directions					
Respects staff and students					
Remains on task					
Other					
ACADEMIC					
TOTAL					

Bathroom _____   TOTAL POINTS _____

Figure 7.2   *Sample of a More Detailed Daily Report*

prove, the improvement shows immediately. For the student who slipped one day, it is noted. Since the feedback is clear, there is little room for misinterpretation. The teacher can be sure that the correct message is received.

There is also included a notation of "Bathroom" on the point sheet. If a student needs a bathroom pass, it is recorded there for all to see. This prevents the student from going to the bathroom from every class or at the end of one period and the start of the next. It's a coordinated approach that is both convenient and simple.

BIRTHDAYS: WE FORGET OURS BUT REMEMBER THEIRS

As we get older, we either try to forget our own birthday or downplay it. Not so with kids. For them, birthdays are a big deal. Everybody celebrates Christmas or Hanukkah, Thanksgiving, and the 4th of July, but a birthday is personal. It's your day and no one else's.

Celebrating birthdays is an important tool in developing a special rapport with your students. And, of course, you celebrate a birthday with a cake. As you know from other sections in this book, I am death on sugar and junk food. But every rule has its exception and the exception to the sugar rule is a birthday cake. Celebrating a birthday with apples and oranges just doesn't do it! Though it can cost you a little time and money, the best way to celebrate birthdays is with an individual cake for each child on his or her birthday. At a convenient time in the school day, perhaps before recess or during homeroom, the class activities stop, the cake with candles is brought in, and everyone sings "Happy Birthday." Although older kids may pooh-pooh it, it really means a lot to them as well.

If individual cakes become prohibitive, you can combine those birthdays occurring in the same week for a weekly celebration, or in the same month for a monthly celebration. Be careful not to forget the kids who had a summer birthday. You can have a special birthday party at the start or end of the year. Birthdays are a very personal celebration for each student. Make sure you are a part of them.

USING THE TAPE RECORDER FOR SELF-EVALUATION

It is very difficult to examine our classroom style while in the middle of it. Having a colleague or two observe and give us some feedback is a good way to provide information for self-evaluation. But such observation can pose problems. When someone else enters the room, both you and the students can subtly change your behaviors. Finding colleagues with the time to observe can be hard. And many of us are insecure when it comes to peer evaluation.

There is another solution. If you place a voice-activated tape recorder in such a way as to capture sounds in the room, you can record a period's worth of verbal interactions. While this will not give as much information as a keen observer could provide, it does give you an unbiased record of verbal interaction within your classroom. When you play back such a recording, you can note your frequency of interactions, types of interactions by pupil/subject/style, and other characteristics of your classroom management.

A video camera might be more effective since it would record non-verbal interactions as well. The problem with video is that it tends to be more intrusive than a tape recorder and has difficulty picking up all parts of the room. Since analysis of management style requires unbiased feedback, using a tape recorder is a good technique in assisting the teacher. The sounds it records are not selective and the use of the recording can be both personal and effective.

CHAPTER 8

Creating a Classroom Management Plan

THE CLASSROOM MANAGEMENT PLAN

The development of a classroom management plan (CMP) requires careful planning. After determining the philosophical approach with which you are most comfortable and the specifics of your classroom situation, you must weigh many factors as a workable classroom plan emerges. This chapter presents a structured approach to the development of such a plan. Since a CMP must be tailored to your individual needs and environment, there are no right or wrong components. Rather, this chapter recognizes you as the best judge of what is good for your classroom and gives you a format by which to approach it. Done in an open and honest fashion, it will provide you with a good base for your classroom management. Take the time to do a thorough job. Tasks can be performed over time—don't feel a need to rush. If the job is approached properly the results will prove meaningful.

TASK 1: STATING YOUR PHILOSOPHICAL BASE

Take time to complete the following statement as honestly as possible. Ponder it fully. Use scratch paper to jot down some options, weighing them carefully before making your final entries. Remember, this document is designed to assist *you* in developing a plan that will be right for *you*. Make it fit!

> **Kids are basically _____ and/but need _____.**
> **Once in a while, however, _____.**

Examine the teacher-student interaction models summarized here:

1. The Supportive Model: Gordon's Teacher Effectiveness Training (TET)   The TET model emphasizes a warm, accepting relationship between teacher and students. Sensitive, warm, and noncritical teachers attempt to help students acquire healthy, positive self-concepts through specific teacher actions and methods.

2. The Communication Model: Berne/Harris's Transactional Analysis (TA)   Teachers and students must decode and analyze messages they send each other to facilitate realistic solutions. TA provides the teacher with a means to decode these messages, teaches students the code, and develops a common framework for student-teacher communications.

3. The Valuing Model: Raths and Simon's Values Clarification   Students need to clarify their values. This allows them to be more consistent and rational in correcting their behaviors. They are provided with a supportive, nonjudgmental environment in which to explore reasons for and internalize freely chosen actions.

4. The Social Discipline Model of Rudolf Dreikurs   Every student wishes to belong. Teachers, by identifying a student's misdirected goal as exhibited by misbehavior, can understand that student's needs. They can counter this misdirected goal with a plan enabling the student to use appropriate behavior to belong successfully.

5. The Reality Model of William Glasser   Although every student has the ability to be rational and responsible, students do not acquire this themselves. Teachers provide a successful classroom of relevant activities and confront students when their behavior prevents success. The student commits to a future plan for success that is reinforced by the teacher.

6. The Behavior Modification Model   Positive reinforcement shapes behavior. Small units of behavior are reinforced through verbal, social, or material rewards. Behavioral standards are uniform and consistent. The system applies to all students, regardless of age or intellectual differences.

7. The Assertiveness Model of Lee and Marlene Canter   In addition to being rewarded for appropriate behaviors, students must be punished for inappropriate behaviors. Teachers must assert their right to teach and develop a plan of rewards and punishments that will reinforce their authority and facilitate learning.

8. The Behaviorism/Punishment Model of Engelmann and Dobson   While positive rewards for appropriate behaviors are important, negative measures (including physical punishment) are needed to punish inappropriate behaviors. While we recognize the need for concern and patience with students, reinforcement of the teacher's authority is critical through a quick and efficient system to deal with disruptive behavior. (For further explanation of these models in one source see Wolfgang and Glickman's *Solving Discipline Problems*, Allyn and Bacon, 1986.)

In light of the list of models presented, answer the following questions:

- Which one model best describes your statement?
- What other models are reflected in your statement?

You may want to read further on the model that best describes your style.

TASK 2: SETTING EXPECTATIONS

It is important that students understand the standards of your classroom. Which behaviors are expected and which are not? List the basic expectations of your classroom. Go back and review your expectations, keeping the following in mind:

- Are they stated so as to set positive expectations for your students?
- Have you covered all-important areas—conduct, academic work, and so forth?
- Are they clear?
- Are they broad enough so as not to be too specific?
- Are they all necessary?

This is *not* an exercise in neatness. Scratch, modify, and edit at will. When you decide your list is final, number the items in priority with number one being the most important.

TASK 3: POSITIVE STROKES

Human development and growth are guided and formed by our interaction with our environment—the people, places, and experiences
with which we live and interact. If we feel good about something, we
tend to repeat it. If we are hurt by something, we tend to avoid it.
This is the basic principle of behavior modification. One could con-
ceivably mold a student's behavior by always punishing his or her
undesirable behaviors. The result, however, would be a very negative environment. As teachers attempting to create a positive learning experience, it is important that we focus our classroom efforts on
recognizing and rewarding appropriate behaviors. Consequently, the
next task in the development of your CMP is just that—how will you
recognize and reward students who have met your classroom expectations?

Educators differ on the topic of student rewards. There is concern
that we should not "buy" student conduct or effort with material (extrinsic) rewards: students should do good for the sake of doing good
(intrinsic rewards). The goal of education is to move students in that direction. It is a developmental process, however, that requires time and
starts extrinsically, as it slowly moves toward the intrinsic.

While it can be a fine distinction at times, working for a reward versus receiving a reward for good work can demonstrate two distinct and
different approaches, as shown in these two examples.

Example 1   For next Monday, each science team will complete and
submit the results of their experiment. The team with the best report
will win a pizza party.

Example 2   I have reviewed and corrected each team's experiment.
There was some very good work from every team, with one team doing an exceptional job. Jerry, Don, and Maria: look for me in the cafeteria for a special treat!

Rather than offering a reward for good conduct or work as in example 1, it "falls from Heaven" as a result of good work as in example 2.
And, as we have learned from B. F. Skinner, when those rewards "fall
from Heaven" on an occasional basis, they are more reinforcing than
those that are continual.

The next section assists you in developing your recognition/reinforcement plan as you complete a table for each expectation. While some tables will be very similar, others may be very different, as you will note in the following examples.

Expectation 1. Students behave themselves as ladies and gentlemen (conduct).

Step	Recognition/Reinforcer	Frequency	De-escalation Plan
1.	Gesture/verbal praise	Ongoing	None
2.	Star on chart	Daily	Weekly after 2nd week
3.	Popcorn/video party	Biweekly	Monthly after Sept.
4.	Field trip	Semester	None

Expectation 2. Students complete their homework assignments correctly and on time (academic).

Step	Recognition/Reinforcer	Frequency	De-escalation Plan
1.	Collect and correct all homework	Daily	None
2.	Place stars on homework chart	Daily	Weekly after 2nd week
3.	Scholar of the Month Certificate	Monthly	None
4.	Field trip	Semester	None

Keep several important ideas in mind as you develop your reward program:

Simple recognition can be an important reinforcer.   The simple act of recognizing good behavior or work can, in and of itself, be sufficient reward: "Well done Mary!" "Good job Mike!" "Wow, José, that was nice!"

Gold stars can be as valuable as gold coins.   While many elementary teachers use stars or stamps as reinforcers, they also work well at the high school and adult level.

Rewards every so often can be far more reinforcing than a reward given every time.   As B. F. Skinner demonstrated with his operant conditioning experiments, partial rewards (once in a while) are more powerful than continual rewards (those given every time).

Many times, the process of giving a reward is more reinforcing than the reward itself.   Again, simple recognition.

Rewards must be honest.   Students know when their work or conduct merits a reward. If a teacher rewards that which does not merit it, the system rapidly loses its value.

Every student can be rewarded.   While the outstanding student might be praised for a perfect score, the struggling student can also be praised when he or she has improved. Behaviors change through successive approximations (small steps in the right direction). Therefore, it is important that we positively recognize each student as he or she *moves toward* improvement.

Develop your positive reinforcement plan, completing the columns in figure 8.1.

Recognition/Reinforcer   In the first column of the table list the cascade of reinforcers you will use as you recognize and reinforce appropriate responses to each expectation. Begin with the simplest reinforcer (a smile, verbal praise). Each succeeding step will increase in value (symbolically, not necessarily monetarily), ending with the last being the most complex (pizza party, trip).

Frequency   In the next column, plan your reward frequency. The simplest reinforcer can be continual—a smile, a word of praise. In each succeeding step as their value increases, their frequency decreases. While the first step is continual, the second might be weekly, the third biweekly, and the last monthly. Remember that smaller children need a greater frequency, while the older students can postpone rewards for a longer period. (Try asking a kindergartener to wait a month for an ice cream.)

De-escalation Plan   To assist students in successfully meeting classroom expectations, they should receive positive responses to their appropriate behaviors. For that reason, it is important that students are given frequent reinforcements/rewards at the beginning of the school year. As a positive classroom milieu is established, and as the group begins to turn to more intrinsic means of self-recognition, the frequency of the extrinsic rewards (those provided by the teacher) may be decreased. In the last column, outline how your reward system could be decreased as your classroom milieu is established.

Expectation 1: _____

Step	Recognition/Reinforcer	Frequency	De-escalation Plan
1.			
2.			
3.			
4.			

Figure 8.1 _Positive Reinforcement Plan_

Expectation 2: _____

Step	Recognition/Reinforcer	Frequency	De-escalation Plan
1.			
2.			
3.			
4.			

Expectation 3: _____

Step	Recognition/Reinforcer	Frequency	De-escalation Plan
1.			
2.			
3.			
4.			

Figure 8.1 Positive Reinforcement Plan (continued)

Expectation 4: _____

Step	Recognition/Reinforcer	Frequency	De-escalation Plan
1.			
2.			
3.			
4.			

Expectation 5: _____

Step	Recognition/Reinforcer	Frequency	De-escalation Plan
1.			
2.			
3.			
4.			

Figure 8.1 *Positive Reinforcement Plan (continued)*

Expectation 6: _____

Step	Recognition/Reinforcer	Frequency	De-escalation Plan
1.			
2.			
3.			
4.			

Note: If you're looking for a space for the seventh expectation, reevaluate. You've got too many. Are they too specific? Can they be logically combined?

TASK 4: NEGATIVE CONSEQUENCES

The most effective part of your classroom management system is your program of rewards and recognition, but there will be times when a student must receive a negative response. In developing your system of negative consequences or punishments, pay close attention to several factors:

Negative consequences should be immediate.   The closer punishment follows the act that precipitated it, the more effective it will be. In effect, you are pairing the negative consequence with the act that precipitated it. While immediacy is not always possible, it should be your goal.

Negative consequences should be handled within your classroom. Each time you leave discipline to an authority outside your classroom, you invite several problems. First, you lose control over the process and can easily have your position inadvertently compromised. Second, you admit a lack of authority in your relationship with the student. And third, punishment is often postponed because of an "office backlog."

Students should see negative consequences as (by definition) unpleasant.   Just because you see an action as negative, don't assume that students interpret it in the same way. Students craving your individualized attention might find staying after school rewarding.

Negative consequences should be consistent and certain.   Just as night follows day, consequences should follow an inappropriate behavior that requires it. If a student occasionally gets away with an inappropriate behavior, he or she will continue to test your system for the chance of getting away with it again.

Plans should include a cascade of increasingly negative consequences.   Your plan should have a "cascade" of consequences. Perhaps the first offense would receive a verbal warning or name on the board. Each succeeding offense would receive a more severe consequence. If an increase in severity of response does not prove effective, a reevaluation of your plan in relation to that student/group should be made. Extremely serious behaviors or repeated behaviors might require intervention starting at a higher step.

Use the following examples and figure 8.2 to design a negative consequence program similar to your reward program. Identify negative consequences in increasing seriousness for each expectation. For purposes of this exercise, any de-escalation would reverse this process.

Expectation 1. Students behave themselves as ladies and gentlemen (conduct)

Step   Schedule of Negative Consequences
1.   Gesture/verbal reprimand
2.   Name on board
3.   Five minutes in quiet corner, or
        Five minutes delay in recess, or
        Five minutes after school
4.   Ten minutes in quiet corner, or
        Ten minutes delay in recess, or
        Twenty minutes after school

Expectation 2. Students complete their homework assignments correctly and on time (academic)

Step   Schedule of Negative Consequences
1.   Name on board until following day when makeup assignment is due.
2.   If repeated during following two weeks, stays after school to complete assignment.
3.   Continued problem, call to parent to enlist their cooperation and supervision of homework.
4.   Continued problem, parent-teacher-student conference.

You will notice a significant difference in the negative consequence schedule for behavioral and academic expectations. With behavior, our objective is to diminish the frequency of negative behavior. With academics, our objective is to facilitate learning through the completion of assignments.

TASK 5: PREPARING YOUR SUPPORT SYSTEMS

Management of your classroom relies on your ability and authority as teacher, but there are times when you will need outside (defined as anything beyond your classroom walls) support for your efforts. Take a moment to write down the various types of groups/persons from whom you may need support. Your list should include parents, school admin-

Expectation 1: _____

Step	Punishment/Negative Consequence Schedule
1.	
2.	
3.	
4.	

Figure 8.2 *Sample Consequence Schedule*

Expectation 2: _____

Step	Punishment/Negative Consequence Schedule
1.	
2.	
3.	
4.	

Expectation 3: _____

Step	Punishment/Negative Consequence Schedule
1.	
2.	
3.	
4.	

Figure 8.2 Sample Consequence Schedule

Expectation 4: _____

Step	Punishment/Negative Consequence Schedule
1.	
2.	
3.	
4.	

Expectation 5: _____

Step	Punishment/Negative Consequence Schedule
1.	
2.	
3.	
4.	

Figure 8.2 Sample Consequence Schedule (continued)

Expectation 6: _____

Step	Punishment/Negative Consequence Schedule		
1.			
2.			
3.			
4.			

Figure 8.2 Sample Consequence Schedule (continued)

istrators, and colleagues. In addition you might list such groups as friends and family who provide for your own personal support, professional organizations, graduate courses, and so forth. When you have completed your list, letter the items starting with A for identification (again, not by priority). Once you have established your support list, you need to begin planning how you will prepare and actuate such support systems when they are needed. Briefly outline your plans in figure 8.3, using the following example as a guide. Please note that the actuation steps are not meant to coincide with preparation phases.

Group A—Parents

Preparation	*Actuation*
Letter explaining management system at opening of school.	Phone call home for positive or negative report.
Explanation of management system at Parent's Night in October.	Note home for positive or negative report.
Update newsletter at beginning of second semester.	Principal/teacher/parent conference, parent conference.

TASK 6: EVALUATION

Even the most perfectly designed system needs ongoing evaluation. Before implementation of your system, it would be helpful to get input from others. Sometimes we become so engrossed in the planning process that we overlook critical components. Further, what may be very simple and understandable to us sends a completely different message to someone else. Evaluations do not have to be elaborate. Sitting with a respected colleague and discussing your reward program may provide you with the necessary feedback. Discussing parent support with your principal may give you added insight as well as allowing the principal to "buy into" your program. Take some time to think how you would get meaningful feedback to your system before its implementation. Describe the group(s) you would use, the format (informal discussion, written critique, meeting) you would follow, and the specific areas you would address with them. Complete figure 8.4, based on the following example.

Group	Preparation	Actuation
A		
B		
C		

Figure 8.3 Support System

D	
E	

Figure 8.3 *Support System (continued)*

**Group(s): Group of friends who are parents
of school-age children
Format: Saturday morning coffee klatch
Areas addressed: Parental support component**

Group(s): _____
Format: _____
Areas addressed: _____

Figure 8.4 Evaluation Form

Also important in an evaluation process is the ongoing evaluation. Once your system is in place, you need a plan of reevaluation. Some of this could involve the groups you outlined above partway through the year. As in the example, you might meet again with the parents group to discuss modifications made to the plan and various problems encountered during implementation.

It is also important that you evaluate the overall results of your classroom management plan during the year. If behavior with certain students continues to deteriorate despite your plan's activities, reevaluation may give you needed ideas for revision.

Sometimes our plans appear excellent on paper but don't click on implementation. Is there something going on within the classroom that has gone unnoticed? We all know the expression of being unable to see the forest for the trees. What support could you call into play to assist you in evaluating the day-to-day operations of your plan? A tape recorder running for a period could give you important aural feedback when replayed that night. Are there trusted colleagues who would be willing to watch your interaction with a specific student during their free period one day? Think about several ways in which you could get feedback on your day-to-day operations. For each problem list the following information:

- Define problem addressed.
- Who's providing feedback?
- How is feedback provided?

TASK 7: TEACHING SOCIAL SKILLS AND VALUES

The development of social skills and values is an important part of every student's education. If these experiences are not presented as part of a planned curriculum, however, they can be easily overlooked.

Take a few minutes to brainstorm the social skills you feel children should develop during their school experience (K-12). Don't edit the list at this point. If it comes to mind, write it down. Sit with some colleagues/fellow students and discuss your list. Use this time to clarify your thinking and to eliminate entries that, on second thought, do not belong. Add any you have overlooked. *Keeping the population and grade level you teach in mind*, go over your list and identify the most important five by numbering them from 1 (highest priority) to 5.

On a sheet of paper divided into two columns, rewrite your priorities for a social skill or value at the top. In the left column, list a variety of classroom activities you might use to teach them. In the right column, develop a tentative time frame for presenting each social skill/value. Use the following as an example.

Priority—The Value of Sharing

Activity	*Timetable*
1. Values clarification exercise	3rd Friday in September
2. Divide students into pairs, assigned to make paper collage. Each pair must share scissors and paste pot. Discuss activity.	4th Friday in September
3. Reinforce sharing behaviors in class	Ongoing

The social skill/values evaluation method is a beginning. Use it as a resource when you develop your lesson plans for the year, including its general structure, activities, and ideas. If you give the table proper attention, your students will develop more appropriate social skills and will have the chance to explore important values within their youthful world.

WHAT NOW?

This exercise has provided you a structure with which to begin the development of a classroom management system. You began by examining your philosophical approach, allowing you to understand the basic premises upon which your system is built. You learned that there are no right or wrong answers. What's right is a system that *you* feel best fits *your* personality and the environment in which you work.

Basic to any behavioral management system are positives (rewards) that recognize those students who have met our expectations, and negatives (punishments) for those who have not. There is an old axiom that we teach as we were taught. This may be very true. But if we continue to reward and punish as we were rewarded and punished, we may miss the mark. As times change, so should our perceptions of what is rewarding and punishing. In years past, suspension from school was almost a death penalty. In today's society, with few parents in the home to supervise a suspension, it has lost its sting. This does not mean to say that old ways of doing things are no longer appropriate. But we need to examine our rewards and punishments carefully to ensure that they are the most appropriate for the age, social maturity, and environment of the students we teach.

Although teachers must develop management systems that are self-supporting, there are times when we must look outside our system for support. Such support needs careful exploration and development *before a crisis develops*. Often we fail to preplan for this need. Your exploration and development of such a support system will be extremely beneficial when the need for it arises. Further, once your support system is in place, it will need periodic maintenance.

Ongoing evaluation is critical to any plan's success. It helps us to work out problems inherent in the plan and allows us to update the plan as times, students, and/or supports change. Through the inclusion of a good evaluation sequence, your plan will remain alive and responsive to the needs of your classroom.

Lastly, it is important that we develop an academic base for the social skills and values that we feel are important. This requires the preparation of a curriculum in this area rather than leaving such learning to chance.

The most important part of this exercise is the thought and attention it has produced. Now that you have completed the various tasks, use your newfound or rediscovered knowledge as a guide to organize, refine, and implement your classroom management plan.

These exercises are designed to provide assistance in the development of a CMP. The same steps and principles can be used to develop a school management plan. Such a plan can be drawn from a compilation of the individual teachers' CMPs, or can be developed first to provide direction for the development of their individual plans.

Good luck!

About the Author

Ray Petty (Ed.D., Nova University) is associate professor of education at the Ponce Campus of the Inter American University of Puerto Rico. For twelve years he was principal of the Special Education Learning Center, a specialized public school (K–12) for 185 behavior-disordered students in Hartford, Connecticut. In addition, he lectures frequently at teacher training programs in colleges and universities, gives in-service programs in public and private schools, and has published many articles in a variety of educational journals. Dr. Petty was recently named a Fulbright Senior Specialist in Education.